ANNETTE LAMING

Annette Laming

LASCAUX

PAINTINGS AND
ENGRAVINGS

TRANSLATED BY

Eleanore Frances Armstrong

PENGUIN BOOKS

Penguin Books Ltd, Harmondsworth, Middlesex
U.S.A.: Penguin Books Inc., 3300 Clipper Mill Road, Baltimore 11, Md
AUSTRALIA: Penguin Books Pty Ltd, 762 Whitehorse Road,
Mitcham, Victoria

—

First published 1959

—

Made and printed in Great Britain
by Richard Clay & Company, Ltd, Bungay, Suffolk
Collogravure plates by Harrison & Sons Ltd

CONTENTS

CONTENTS

LIST OF PLATES

7

Thanks are due to the following for permission to reproduce photographs for this volume: Plates 1–16, 18–35, and 41–3, the Archives Photographiques, Caisse National des Monuments Historiques, Paris; Plate 38, Carl Nesjar, Larvik, Norway. Plate 40, Photo Reportage Yan, Toulouse; Plate 44, Photo Rivière Sarlat; and Plates 46–7, Professor F. E. Zeuner of the Institute of Archaeology, University of London.

LIST OF TEXT FIGURES

The original drawings in this book are not copies; some are reproductions of sketches made in the cave, some are reproductions of sketches made from a selection of photographs taken from various angles, and others are combinations of both. *Their sole purpose is to illustrate the text.*

LIST OF TABLES

EDITORIAL FOREWORD

BY

Wilfrid J. M. Synge

Lascaux is the first volume of a series planned to cover a number of important themes related to that particular period known as the Old Stone Age or the Palaeolithic. Each volume will be written by a specialist who will be free to decide the most significant and interesting aspects of the subject with which he is dealing. The planning of the series requires careful consideration, for the field is a large one, but the aim is to form an intelligent and valuable guide to the Old Stone Age in many of its phases. The immediate intention is to produce a second volume on the theme of prehistoric cave art which will deal with the famous cave at *Altamira* in Northern Spain, where authentic paintings and engravings of Upper Palaeolithic man were discovered for the first time by Don Marcelino S. du Sautuola in 1879.

In this book Annette Laming has set out for our benefit the results of many years of study of Man's earliest known works of art, and of her research into the origin and purpose of these paintings and engravings which, in a large number of underground caves in France and Spain, record for us the vision of a world long vanished. It is important to remember, as the author has been careful to remind us, that although the psychology of Upper Palaeolithic man may not have differed greatly from our own, mere aesthetics – 'Art for Art's sake' – which may have played a vital part in the decoration of personal objects such as lamps, spear-throwers, etc., is not the dominant motive in cave art itself. The hunter artist would not have taken the trouble to acquire and develop his wonderful artistic skill and devote it to the decoration of almost inaccessible parts of the cave unless he had some ulterior purpose to serve. What that purpose was is not yet fully understood despite half a century of research; hunting ritual and the practice of sympathetic magic do not appear to provide a satisfactory answer to this perplexing, but fascinating question. Many other problems remain, requiring further evidence before they can be resolved. Meanwhile, *Lascaux* is both a concise guide for those who intend to visit this world-famous cave, and a valuable reference book for the student of Palaeolithic art.

The line drawings in this book are the result of careful work by Miss Lavinia Buswell, under the direction of the author, and we are greatly indebted to Professor F. E. Zeuner for permission to reproduce the paintings appearing on Plates 46 and 47, and to Professor Lutz Heck of Wiesbaden for placing at our disposal the photograph reproduced on Plate 48a.

THE CAVE SANCTUARIES OF PREHISTORY

Discoveries and Areas of Distribution

THE first example of Palaeolithic art – an engraving of hinds on a fragment of bone – was discovered about 1834 in the cave of Chaffaud (Vienne). Its great antiquity was not recognized at the time, for there was still great doubt whether 'antediluvian man' had in fact ever existed; and the possibility of there having been an artistic culture at such a remote epoch had never been considered at all. Rapid progress was made in the study of Prehistory, however, and by the middle of the nineteenth century the co-existence of man with the large extinct fauna was conclusively established. At the same time discoveries of examples of Palaeolithic art constantly increased in number and provided further decisive proof of the great antiquity of man, for it was clear that the artists who had depicted reindeer and mammoth on bone and stone must have lived in Western Europe at the same time as these animals. The excavations of Lartet and Christy, begun in 1861 in the region of Les Eyzies, and in particular the discovery at the site of La Madeleine of a piece of ivory engraved with the unmistakable figure of a mammoth, proved once and for all that the numerous engravings and sculptures found at these sites dated from the Old Stone Age.

As the years passed, discoveries of engraved bone fragments multiplied; but as yet there was no thought of connecting these with the engravings and paintings of animals on the walls of caves which were beginning to be announced. Certain paintings, for example those in the cave of Rouffignac in the Dordogne, had been known for some hundreds of years, but they had apparently never aroused any especial interest. In 1864 Dr Garrigou visited the cave of Niaux, whose paintings, particularly those in the *Salon noir*, have now long been recognized as masterpieces of Quaternary art and could not fail to attract the attention of even the most uninformed visitor. Nevertheless, although he had just explored the rock shelter of Bruniquel in the Tarn, and was therefore aware of the existence of a Palaeolithic art, he merely made the following entry in his diary: 'There are some paintings on the wall: what on earth can they be?'

Fifteen years later, in 1879, a Spanish archaeologist, Don Marcelino S. de Sautuola, explored the cave of Altamira for the second time. His little daughter, who was playing beside him in the cave, suddenly called out to him that she saw some bulls on the ceiling. Sautuola looked up and, to his utter amazement, saw that there were indeed numerous painted and engraved animals distributed in wild confusion on the vaulted ceiling above his head: a horse, a large hind, and numbers of bison in a variety of attitudes. He immediately examined the inner galleries of the cave, where he found many more paintings.

Sautuola never doubted the extreme antiquity of the paintings; but, though supported by Juan Vilanova y Piera in Spain and Piette in France, his theories were utterly rejected by a sceptical scientific world. For a brief while, it is true, the curiosity of prehistorians was aroused; but they soon lost interest in the matter and it was not even mentioned at the International Congress of Prehistoric Archaeology and Anthropology held at Lisbon only a year after the discovery. For a long time the only account in France of Altamira was to be found in Édouard Harlé's report published in 1882.* Harlé had visited the cave and, after a careful examination, had come to the conclusion that the polychrome paintings of the Great

---

* Harlé (Ed.), 'La Grotte d'Altamira près de Santander (Espagne)', *Matériaux pour l'histoire de l'homme*, 1882–3, 17ᵉ année, pp. 275–83.

Hall were indisputably of very recent date and had probably been executed between Sautuola's two visits to the cave – that is between 1875, when he never noticed any paintings at all, and 1879, when he discovered them. As for the other paintings in the cave, Harlé maintained that they were certainly not of the same date as the archaeological remains, although they might be a little earlier than the paintings in the Great Hall. In his report he included an illustration of some geometrical designs and a very crude silhouette of an animal selected from among the most primitive figures in the entire cave because he considered that its very crudity proved it to be of earlier date than the others. This was the first time that a figure from a Palaeolithic wall-painting had ever been published in France, but it aroused little interest: Altamira was forgotten almost as soon as it was discovered.

Years passed, and then, in 1895, at a meeting of the Académie des Sciences, Émile Rivière reported the discovery of certain paintings and engravings on the walls of the cave of La Mouthe near Les Eyzies which he ascribed to prehistoric cultures. He too met only with scepticism. Nevertheless, such discoveries increased in number. In 1896 the engravings at Pair-non-Pair in the Gironde were reported, and in 1897 the paintings at Marsoulas in the Haute Garonne. At the same time it was recalled that as early as 1878 a schoolmaster named Chiron had discovered some 'incised figures' on the walls of the cave of Le Chabot in the Gard and had had them photographed, but his find had aroused no interest. At last, in 1901, when Les Combarelles and Font-de-Gaume' in the Dordogne near the prehistoric centre of Les Eyzies were discovered within a few months of each other, the antiquity of cave art was generally recognized and these masterpieces of prehistoric art were duly acclaimed. The authenticity of all the discoveries so far made was then conclusively established, and Émile Cartailhac, one of the eminent prehistorians of the day, who had been among the first to deny the antiquity of the paintings at Altamira, now made a point of publicly recognizing the cave which he had previously done so much to discredit and condemn to oblivion. His 'Mea Culpa of a Sceptic', published in 1902 in *L'Anthropologie*, marked the end of the experimental stage in the study of prehistoric cave art.

Since the beginning of this century discoveries of painted caves and shelters have been made at comparatively regular intervals and they are still being made today. The following are among the most important: Hornos de la Pena and Castillo, discovered in 1906; Le Portel in 1908; Le Cap Blanc and Laussel in 1909; La Pasiega and La Pileta in 1911; Les Trois Frères in 1916; Pech-Merle in 1922; and the sculptured frieze of Roc de Sers in 1927. In 1940 the entrance to the cave of Lascaux was discovered quite by chance. The paintings in this cave are among the most beautiful and the best preserved examples of cave art yet discovered; they have aroused a new interest in the subject of Palaeolithic art and excited the curiosity and admiration of large numbers of the general public as well as the attention of archaeologists and prehistorians.

In recent years many fresh discoveries have been made as a result of the prevailing enthusiasm for speleology and the increased exploration of caves. In the Dordogne the caves of Gabillou (1941) and Barabao (1951) were explored and their figures deciphered, and very recently (1956) paintings and engravings were re-discovered in the cave of Rouffignac. In the Lot a new gallery in the cave of Pech-Merle was opened up in 1949; and in 1952 some extremely interesting examples of Palaeolithic art were found in the cave of Cougnac. In the Ariège engravings were deciphered in the caves of Ebbou (1946) and Colombier (1947); and in 1946 it became possible to penetrate the galleries of the Grotte du Cheval at Arcy-sur-Cure in the Yonne. In the Vienne the sculptured frieze of Angles-sur-Anglin was brought to light in 1949, and that of the Grotte de la Magdeleine in the Tarn in 1952.

The practice of cave art dates from the final stages of the last glacial period. The artists were the hunters of the Late Palaeolithic era who also displayed great skill in decorating their weapons of bone and ivory with fine engravings and in carving remarkable figurines in stone. *Art mobilier* * and cave art belong to the same period in the history of mankind and show marked similarities of style and technique; but the areas of distribution of these two forms of art do not wholly correspond. In a sense, therefore, they belong to different cultures. For example, the small statuettes known as 'Aurignaciennes' are dispersed over a great part of Eurasia: Aurignacian 'Venuses' have been found in France, Italy, Central Europe, and even as far east as Siberia. Engravings and carvings in low relief on bone and ivory, almost invariably of animals, are distributed over a smaller area. The centre of the area of distribution appears to have been Western Europe – particularly the south-west of France; but traces of this form of art have been found to the north in Belgium and the region of the Meuse; to the south in Spain and Italy; and to the east in Switzerland and as far away as the Ukraine.

The distribution area of cave art can be limited more precisely to the south-west of Europe (Fig. 1). The painted caves of this area fall into three geographical groups.† The first and northernmost group is centred around the valley of the Vézère: Pair-non-Pair in the Gironde, Teyjat and Gabillou in the Dordogne, and the shelters and caves of the Charente and the Vienne belong to this group. In the valley of the Vézère there is an exceptional concentration of painted caves containing a vast number of masterpieces, the finest of which are

---

* *Art mobilier*. Since there is no convenient equivalent in English, this term is used to describe various statuettes and figurines, engraved or sculptured fragments of bone, ivory, or stone, and a variety of decorated objects such as weapons, lamps, etc., found in prehistoric rock-shelters, cave-mouths, or on open sites.

† The painted rock-shelters in Eastern Spain can possibly be dated to the Palaeolithic, but the style of these paintings distinguishes them clearly from Franco-Cantabrian art and they do not come within this classification.

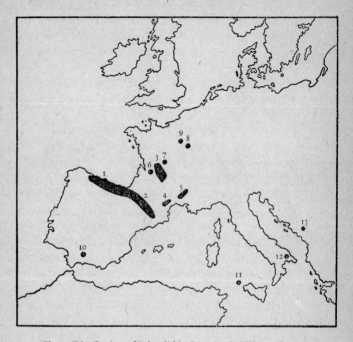

Fig. 1. Distribution of Palaeolithic Cave Art in Western Europe.

[Key] 1 and 2. The Cantabrian mountains and the Pyrenees.
      3. The Dordogne, the Charente, and the Lot.
      4. The Aude and the Hérault.
      5. The Gard and the Ardèche.

Isolated discoveries in the following regions are marked by a dot:
      6. The Gironde.
      7. The Vienne.
      8. The Yonne.
      9. The Forest of Fontainebleau.
     10. The province of Malaga.
     11. The Isle of Levanzo.
     12. Otranto.
     13. Cattaro.

situated within a radius of less than 20 miles from Les Eyzies. Outstanding among these works of art are the bison of Font-de-Gaume, the horses of Les Combarelles, the sculptures of Le Cap Blanc and Laussel, the mammoths of Rouffignac, and the huge friezes of Lascaux. The painted caves of the Lot, which are not far distant from those of the Dordogne, bear a closer resemblance in style to the caves of the Pyrenees – particularly to the cave of Le Portel.

The second group, more important both numerically and in extent, is distributed over the region covering the range of the Pyrenees and the Cantabrian mountains. On the Spanish side lie the caves of Altamira (the most impressive and the first to be discovered), Castillo, Pindal, and La Pasiega. This Spanish group extends southwards as far as Andalusia. On the French side the caves of Niaux, Gargas, Marsoulas, Les Trois Frères, Le Tuc d'Audoubert, Le Portel, and Bédeilhac are among the best known.

The caves in the departments of the Gard, the Ardèche, the Hérault, and the Aude form a third group which is much less rich than the others and which has slightly different characteristics. The most important are Ebbou, Le Figuier, and Chabot.

This area of distribution, originally limited to Spain and Southern France, has been considerably extended by the discoveries of the last few years. About 1905 some rudimentary engravings were found in the cave of Romanelli (Otranto, Italy), but the experts paid scant attention to them and they were not studied until many years later, when they were accepted as being related to Franco-Cantabrian cave art. Very recently some cave engravings forming a link between the designs of the Romanelli cave and those of the Rhône valley have been discovered in the little isle of Levanzo, a few miles off the coast of Sicily.

Fresh discoveries have also been made further north. In 1946, in the Grotte du Cheval at Arcy-sur-Cure, engravings of mammoths, cervids, a bovid, and a horse were deciphered; in 1949 an unpublished Magdalenian painting was reported in one of the innumerable shelters of the Forest of Fontaine-bleau; and more recently still (May 1955) a new discovery in the same area was announced in the Press. The greater the distance from the centre of Franco-Cantabrian cave art, however, the rarer become the discoveries. A few red dots have been found in a cave in Moravia, an engraving of a fish at Cattaro in Yugoslavia, and some engraved slabs in Belgium.* These isolated discoveries extend the area of Palaeolithic cave art far to the north, the east, and the south, but none of them can compare with the masterpieces of France and Spain; Périgord and the region of the Pyrenees were undoubtedly the undisputed centres of influence in the development and expansion of cave art.

Characteristics of Cave Art

Palaeolithic cave art, whether in the Pyrenees, the Périgord, or Provence, is characterized by both great variety and definite homogeneity. The Quaternary artists used many different methods. They painted in outline or in flat wash, in mono-chrome or in polychrome; they made crude finger tracings in soft clay; deep and shallow engravings of delicate or crude design; they sculptured by making use of natural surface irregu-larities, or by cutting away the rock-face; they carved in low relief or in the round and modelled in clay. Their creative achievements range from the most delicate engravings, such as those of the Grotte des Trois Frères, to imposing paintings like the frieze of enormous bulls at Lascaux. They are found on lumps of rock and on the walls of open shelters; in the vast halls of caves and in their innermost and narrowest galleries. Nevertheless, in spite of the complexity and variety of Palaeo-lithic art, a definite homogeneity is apparent in the choice of

* H. Breuil, *Four Hundred Centuries of Cave Art*, pp. 24–5.

subject, the composition, the realism of the execution, and the extreme crudity of the raw materials.

A medley of horses, wild oxen, reindeer, ibexes, bison, and long massive columns of mammoths, lions, bears, and rhinoceroses loom up from the depths of the caves; it is primarily this fauna, extinct in our regions for thousands of years and now resuscitated for us in these paintings, which gives to Quaternary art its consistent character. Cave art is essentially an animal art; whether expressed in paintings, engravings, or sculptures, in huge friezes or the most delicate tracings, it is always – or nearly always – inspired by the animal world. But the hunter-artists did not depict all the animals they knew: they selected those which must have played a large part in the minds and thoughts of the community, particularly the animals they hunted. They portrayed horses or oxen which provided excellent food; lions which were dangerous and had to be killed; and others whose tusks or antlers supplied needs now long forgotten. Hyaenas, wolves, seals, reptiles, fishes, and birds are seldom portrayed.

Quaternary animal art is fundamentally realistic and the animals are portrayed in their customary attitudes. The execution is sometimes clumsy and the poses are often rigid, but the animals are also shown grazing, running, and leaping:

Fig. 2. Remains of a frieze of engraved and painted ibexes' heads at the entrance to the Main Gallery. Only the engraved lines are reproduced in this drawing. With some difficulty a small animal near the middle of the group on the right can be deciphered. Height 1 ft 4 in.

always the artists strove to represent them as they really were and rarely depicted them in a schematized or stylized manner. It is true that the polychrome bison of Font-de-Gaume or Altamira and the frieze of ibex heads at Lascaux (Plates 26 and 27 and Fig. 2), for example, show the beginnings of a stylization: the humps of the former and the long horns of the latter provided tempting subjects indeed for the brush or burin of the artist, and our remote ancestors did not fail to take every advantage of these characteristics and exaggerate and emphasize them. But this stylization was usually extremely restrained, for its sole aim was to make the animals appear true to life: there was no attempt at any form of symbolism. And does not the mere act of representation, even for a photographer, always imply some element of stylization, if only in the choice of a subject or its attitude?

Examples of realistic animal portrayal are to be found in almost all painted and engraved caves. The bearded horse at Niaux (Plate 40) is one of the finest of the paintings; the bovids of Bourdeilles are among the finest examples of sculpture, and the horses of Les Combarelles or the bovids of Teyjat (Fig. 4, see page 37) among the finest engravings. All these examples belong to the second phase of Palaeolithic art.

There are, however, some exceptions to this rule of realism. The two spotted horses and the schematic bisons in the cave of Pech-Merle (Plate 38), the bison of Marsoulas, the so-called 'duckbill' horses in the cave of Le Portel all show a definite stylization, the purpose of which is not clear. One or two of the horses at Lascaux, like those of Le Portel or Pech-Merle, are more or less microcephalic, and the flattened muzzles bear little resemblance to the nostrils of a horse. In some caves there are also representations of imaginary animals, the significance of which is as yet uncertain.

In contrast with the great number of animal figures in cave art, there are notably few portrayals of any form of vegetation. The long branching stem painted in dark ochre on a wall at

Lascaux and the creeper or feather(?) engraved in another hall of the same cave are rare examples; and even these interpretations of the two designs are doubtful. Long branching stems are also present at Marsoulas, though these designs may represent harpoons. Representations of vegetation are as rare in *art mobilier* as they are in cave art.

Portrayals of human figures are likewise few and far between. Some of them are hybrid, with an animal head on a human body, and are often interpreted as masked human figures; but they may represent mythical ancestors. These portrayals are frequently unskilful. The clumsy execution of the masked human figures at Font-de-Gaume, for example, is in striking contrast with the skilful portrayal of the polychrome bison in this cave. This contrast between clumsiness and skill frequently occurs in Palaeolithic art. The Dead Man of Lascaux (Plate 35), for example, is painted in a completely different style from that of the animals around him, and a similar difference of style is noticeable in the human figures at Les Combarelles, the Sorcerer of Pech-Merle, the human silhouettes at Altamira and Le Portel, etc. There are, however, some exceptions. The semi-human figures of the cave of Les Trois Frères, typically Magdalenian in style, are very skilfully and carefully drawn. There are also a few sites in the Périgord with human figures in low relief which are entirely different from the crude stylized figures at Lascaux, Font-de-Gaume, or Les Combarelles. These low reliefs – such as those at Angles-sur-Anglin or at Laussel (Plate 44) – were clearly inspired by very different motives from those which inspired the paintings and engravings, and they belong to an entirely separate artistic group.

In many caves animal figures are often accompanied by signs of doubtful significance, although in some cases these can be interpreted as darts transfixing the animals or as harpoons aimed at them. The precise meaning of the series of red or black dots and the various geometrical signs known as pectiforms, tectiforms, scalariforms, etc., remains obscure. These signs play an important part in the various theories which seek to interpret cave art, but it is not known whether they are symbols or representations of schematized objects – huts, snares, 'blazons', or other unknown products of the Stone Age industry.

In cave art there is a distinct uniformity in the arrangement and presentation of the subject. No attempt was made to indicate scenery or background, although irregularities of the rock surface might be used to suggest ground or water-lines. These instances are rare, however. At Lascaux a natural ledge in the rock-face has been used to suggest the slightly ruffled surface of a river or pool in which deer are swimming (Plates 33 and 42), and in several parts of the cave the animals' feet have been placed on a ledge or natural fold of the rock suggesting a ground line (see Plate 1). Nevertheless, these more or less suggestive representations cannot be regarded as settings in the true sense of the word; and, in any event, although there may sometimes have been an attempt to make use of natural surfaces, no deliberate effort to indicate vegetation, a horizon, or any kind of landscape was ever made.*

The animal figures are almost invariably scattered on the naked rock-face without any respect for proportion. At La Mouthe, for example, an ibex and a mammoth of identical size have been drawn side by side; at Lascaux a brown bear is shown ensconced between the legs of an immense black-spotted bull (Plate 7); and at Cap Blanc two small bison are amply contained between the legs of one of the sculptured horses. In the astonishing network of engravings at Les Trois Frères, exquisite ibexes a few centimetres in size are shown on the same panel as much larger reindeer, bison, and horses, and an enormous bovid literally bestraddles the scene. In some in-

* Below the engravings in the cave of Rouffignac Abbé Breuil has reported a series of small parallel hatchings incised on the cornice. These may represent grass or brushwood.

stances this lack of proportion is due to the fact that the figures are of different styles and belong to various periods of artistic development, but in others the figures are contemporaneous. Even when the artists executed all the figures at the same time as part of an integral composition, they sometimes completely disregarded the respective proportions of these subjects. Animals of the most diverse species are often haphazardly juxtaposed, or superposed one on the other regardless – or so it seems at first to our uninitiated eyes – of order or perspective.

At first sight such an artistic conception is bound to shock those like ourselves who are accustomed to a rationalized form of art – a classic striving after symmetry and harmony, or a total disregard of both. Nevertheless, it should not be forgotten that, amidst the confusion and superpositions so constantly stressed, it is possible to single out groups or friezes of animals of the same species portrayed in identical or similar styles and techniques which produce an astonishing effect of unity. Among the most striking examples are the friezes of ponies, stags, ibexes, and bovids at Lascaux; the bison at Font-de-Gaume or Altamira; the horses at Le Cap Blanc and the various black animals at Niaux. Each of these groups was conceived and executed as a single unit.

It has often been pointed out that, in contrast with the numerous examples of decorative subjects, there is an almost total absence of narrative scenes; indeed, the only instance in the entire cave art of the Valley of the Vézère would appear to be the group in the shaft of the Dead Man at Lascaux (Plate 38), which is so unusual that the authenticity of this painting has sometimes been doubted. The frieze at Le Roc which depicts a man charged by a musk ox may also record some incident in remote antiquity. The most unmistakable scene in the whole of cave art, however, is depicted on an engraving at Les Trois Frères (Ariège) deciphered by Abbé Breuil. On one of the panels of the cave, a semi-human figure which appears to be playing a musical bow and following two very curious creatures is depicted in the midst of a confusion of animal shapes. The figure has a bison's head, but the back, legs, and phallus are human. The arms, which could be accepted as human, end in bison's hoofs, and the long tail is tipped with a tuft of hair. It is preceded by two figures portrayed on the same scale – a bison-headed animal with the body of a hind and a reindeer whose forelegs end in webbed feet. A few groups of male and female animals and parents shown with their young may perhaps be legitimately regarded as narrative scenes, but in addition to these interpretations, other animal associations undoubtedly represent scenes which have not yet been fully deciphered.

The impression of unity produced by the preponderance of animal figures, a certain homogeneity of style and composition, and the recurring presence of numerous symbols not yet fully understood is strengthened by the almost unvarying underground location of the paintings and engravings, by the extreme crudity of all the raw materials used, and by the limestone rock-face, sometimes bare, sometimes covered with calcite, or more rarely with a thin coating of clay, which served the Palaeolithic artists as a canvas. The few modellings in clay which are found only in the French Pyrenees form but an infinitesimal part of the pattern of Quaternary art.

The bare rock-face, unprepared and unsmoothed, played in fact an almost active part in the creation of cave art; its irregularities, depressions, cracks, and ledges, its interplay of hollows and reliefs, far from hampering the artists, would seem to have guided and inspired them. Indeed, the natural contours of the rock, suggesting sometimes the rump, sometimes the belly or the trunk of an animal, and sometimes even the entire beast, often seem to have been the essential inspiration of a composition.

Countless examples can be cited, but neither drawing nor photograph can ever do justice to the evocative power of the rock walls of a cave. Without having spent long hours at a stretch in Palaeolithic caves examining the surfaces of the walls by the uncertain gleam of some fitful light and allowing one's whole being to be overcome by the silence and the dark, it is impossible to realize the extent to which the caves themselves guided the hands and fired the imaginations of those Quaternary artists. Some evocative projection, some play of shadow on the rock-face, has often been a decisive factor in the selection of a subject and its position. The horse's head on the right of the large panel in the cave of Pech-Merle (Plate 38) is formed almost in entirety by a natural indentation in the rock; the contours of the bison at Altamira are strangely delineated by the irregularities of the rocky vault; the rump and a leg of one of the horses at Font-de-Gaume are entirely formed by a stalactite; at Arcy-sur-Cure the legs and trunk of a mammoth seem to emerge from massive stalactite formations; the muzzle, forehead, ears, and humped back of the little brown bear in the Hall of the Bulls at Lascaux are outlined by the irregularities of the rock wall (Plate 8); and at Le Portel a projecting stalactite forms the enormous phallus of a human figure.

In addition to this use of a common canvas, the rock-face, a uniform technique was employed by the Palaeolithic artists. Engravings or incisions were invariably made with a flint burin and are clearly distinguishable from those made with a metal implement. In the case of a painting, though different methods of applying the paint were used (thick or liquid paint was spread with the fingers, a brush, or a pad, or perhaps even sprayed by means of a primitive blower), the colouring matter was always based on ochre for the reds, yellows, and browns, and on oxide of manganese for the blacks and the very dark browns. These colourings are present in Palaeolithic paintings from the Périgord to the South of Spain and impart to all of them a family likeness.

Dating and Evolution

The name of Abbé Henri Breuil has been associated with every important study on Palaeolithic art since the beginning of the twentieth century. We are indebted to him for the copies he has made with careful exactitude of the figures in the principal caves of Franco-Cantabria – his deciphering of the maze of engravings in the cave of Les Trois Frères is particularly remarkable – and for the formulation of a chronology of the principal stages of cave art which constitutes an indispensable basis for any study on Quaternary art.*

My own research into the meaning of cave art has lead me to the belief that many of the superimpositions or juxtapositions of animal figures generally considered to be haphazard and fortuitous should, in fact, be regarded as deliberate associations of particular animals with others.†

Should this theory be verified and accepted, it would tend to regroup some of the stages formulated by Abbé Breuil for any particular cave, and consequently to simplify his table of the development of cave art. Whatever path future research may follow, however, this chronological table formulated by the acknowledged authority on Palaeolithic art after half a century's frequentation and study of the caves represents the starting point which any study of Quaternary art must be developed. The pages which follow are an exposition of the accepted facts on the dating and evolution of cave art based to a great extent on the work of Abbé Breuil, in part on the results of excavations, and in part on the study of the superpositions of the paintings and engravings.

* *Hommage à l'Abbé Breuil* (Paris 1957) contains a complete bibliography of his works on Palaeolithic art.

† *La Signification de l'art rupestre paléolithique.* Thesis for doctorate. (In the press.)

EXCAVATIONS

The mere fact that figures on cave walls and ceilings co-exist with archaeological levels is not sufficient to establish conclusively that both these traces of occupation were contemporaneous: the cave could have been inhabited long before or long after the artists had practised their skill. In order to be able to prove a link in time between wall-paintings and remains of various industries, stratigraphic connexions between them must be established. These connexions always consist of a later superposition on an earlier one, although certain variations may occur. It may sometimes happen that paintings or engravings are discovered in a cave whose entrance, within living memory, has always been blocked with débris in which archaeological deposits have been found *in situ*. In this case the paintings and engravings in the interior of the cave will be at least as early in date as the most recent of the layers blocking the entrance. There are also instances of the lower part of a figure, or even a complete figure (e.g. the sculptured reindeer of Isturitz), being found covered over by archaeological deposits. In this case the figure depicted is obviously of earlier date than the successive archaeological layers covering it.

The earliest stratigraphic dating of cave art was established by Daleau in 1896, when he was excavating the cave of Pairnon-Pair, which was almost entirely filled up with undisturbed deposits. After the entrance was cleared, some rather crude engravings were uncovered, although he did not notice them for some time. These engravings were clearly older than part at least of the filling. Within the cave Daleau recognized a Magdalenian deposit approximately 7 ft 6 in. thick overlying Mousterian deposits 5 ft thick from which it was separated by a thin Solutrean level of about 1 ft. As the engravings were covered by Magdalenian and not Mousterian deposits, Daleau concluded that they dated from the Solutrean or the early Magdalenian era.* This evidence was not conclusive, however, since, from the stratigraphic point of view, the engravings in the cave could arbitrarily have been given as early a date as desired.

In the course of years, owing to frost or other natural causes, the rock-face flaked, or pieces of rock bearing fragments of painting or engraving fell from the decorated walls of a cave. Archaeological deposits continuously formed around these pieces and soon covered them completely, thereby dating their fall, since this obviously occurred before the deposits covered them. A carefully conducted excavation will easily determine the level on which such a piece of rock fell and thus the latest possible date of its fall and its decoration. The age of a large slab painted with a black cervid (Fig. 3c) which had fallen from the ceiling of the Labatut shelter at Sergeac and lay between two Perigordian levels was determined in this way. The painting on the slab was earlier than the formation of the most recent deposit and was accordingly attributed to the earliest Perigordian level. In the neighbouring shelter of Blanchard, a block bearing traces of red and black bovids that had fallen from the ceiling was found in a late Perigordian level. It must be stressed that although in such cases the time of the block's fall can be assigned to a date within the period of the levels between which it lies, there is nothing to fix the time of its decoration, which could be attributed to any early date.

Similar deductions can be made from a study of the degree of deterioration of the ceilings. During the course of an excavation at the Poisson rock shelter in the charming little valley of the Gorge d'Enfer near Les Eyzies, it was found that an entire layer of thin pieces of limestone had crumbled from the ceiling; the fragments lay scattered all around, even below the

* It is to be noted that, as far as early excavations are concerned, Solutrean and Magdalenian designations are always subject to revision, for the Aurignacian era was not classified by Abbé Breuil until 1906, and the Perigordian by D. Peyrony until some time between 1930 and 1940. Cf. Malvesin-Fabre, Société Linnéenne de Bordeaux, 12 January 1946.

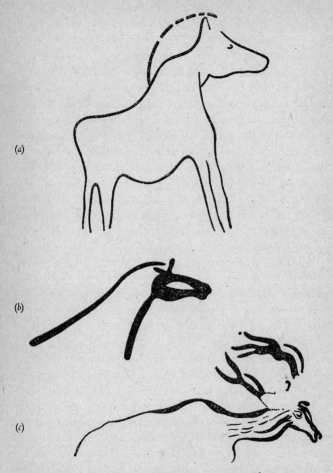

Fig. 3. Perigordian paintings and engravings stratigraphically dated:
(a) Horse engraved on a slab found in the Labatut shelter.   Length 2 ft 3 in.
(b) Head and shoulders of a horse painted on a plaquette, cave of Parpallo, Spain. Upper Perigordian.
(c) Head and shoulders and dorsal line of a deer, Labatut shelter. Upper Perigordian. Length 1 ft 4 in.

large fish sculptured on the ceiling which has given its name to the shelter. As the figure of the fish itself showed no signs of any deterioration, it can be concluded with certainty that it was executed after the crumbling of the roof. This example is interesting, because it is one of the few which establish a maximum age. The figure is undoubtedly of later date than the archaeological layers covered by the pieces of limestone: it is probably of the same date as the upper Perigordian V level.

These applications of the stratigraphic method of dating cave art depend on fortuitous circumstances of rare occurrence, since most of this art is found deep in the interior of the caves, far beyond the archaeological levels at the entrance. In the region of Les Eyzies the only examples of stratigraphic dating are the shelters of Blanchard, Labatut, and Le Poisson, and the frieze of Le Cap Blanc, which was partly covered by an early Magdalenian level.

Other forms of art related to cave art exist, although they are not found on the walls of caves. One form might be classified as 'rock art', for it is mainly represented by sculptures executed on limestone blocks and ranging in size from approximately 8 inches to a yard or more. These sculptures can be dated in the same way as any other remains, since they are found in archaeological levels. The most accurately dated examples are the sculptured frieze of Le Roc, which is Solutrean; the bovids of Bourdeilles, which are also Solutrean; the human figures at Laussel (Plate 44), attributed to Magdalenian or sometimes to the end of the Perigordian; and the sculptures of Angles-sur-Anglin, which are early Magdalenian. The very crude paintings and engravings of La Ferrassie, which are Aurignacian in date and perhaps represent the beginnings of Palaeolithic art, are also executed on detached blocks. Unfortunately, the exact chronological and cultural relationship of these sculptured blocks to cave art in general is not known. It is probable that the sculptures are of the same date as a certain number of cave paintings, but they were inspired by very different motives; and the chronological indications provided by these isolated examples are not applicable to the majority of the paintings.

TABLE I

PRINCIPAL STRATIGRAPHIC DATINGS OF WALL ART

Sites	Cultures	Characteristics of the Art
La Ferrassie	Aurignacian III and IV	Stiff engravings Traces of painting Crude red-and-black animals
Pair-non-Pair	Aurignacian (?) or Perigordian (?)	Stiff engravings
Labatut Shelter	Minimum age: Perigordian V	Very stiff engraving of a horse Hand encircled with black Red-and-black animals underlying animals in black line
Blanchard Shelter	Minimum age: Perigordian V	Red animals thickly outlined in black
The Poisson Shelter	Maximum age: Perigordian IV	⎫
Le Roc	Solutrean	⎪
Bourdeilles	Solutrean	⎪
Isturitz	Solutrean–Beginning of Magdalenian IV	⎬ Sculptures
Laussel	Early Magdalenian	⎪
Angles-sur-Anglin	Early Magdalenian	⎪
Cap Blanc	Minimum age: Magdalenian III	⎭
Teyjat	Minimum age: Magdalenian V	Delicate engravings

In actual fact, if the sculptures and the sculptured blocks are considered as a separate group, examples of cave art which can be dated stratigraphically are very limited; but the clues which they provide are none the less valuable. The earliest come from La Ferrassie. In the Aurignacian levels, flakes of rock that had fallen from the roof and which bore traces of red and black pigment representing perhaps a cervid and an ibex (Aurignacian III) were found, together with fragments of slabs either painted or engraved with crude and stiff silhouettes: a lion(?), the head of a rhinoceros(?), the hindquarters, some legs, and a belly of some barely distinguishable creatures (Aurignacian IV). As no work of art has ever been discovered in an early Perigordian level, these few remains are considered to be traces of the hunter-artists' first rudimentary efforts. The engraved silhouettes of Pair-non-Pair are also classified as Aurignacian, because the lower parts were covered by archaeological deposits probably dating from the Aurignacian period. The excavations of Pair-non-Pair were undertaken at the end of the nineteenth century, however, when the Aurignacian industry had not yet been identified. A study of the tools from this site, made many years after it had been excavated, proves that above the Mousterian level the cave contained several Aurignacian and Perigordian levels which had previously been classified as Magdalenian. In the circumstances it is impossible to verify the exact level at which the engravings ended, and, though they may be Aurignacian, in the absence of clear stratigraphy, it is impossible to be sure.

The Perigordian levels in the Labatut rock shelter contained several blocks which had fallen from the roof (Figs. 3a and c). One of these bears a deep engraving of a horse with a very elongated head; on another there is a hand encircled with black. A third is painted with two groups of figures: the underlying series is composed of large animals outlined in black and filled in with red; the superposed figures, more modest in size, are drawn entirely in black outline. In the Blanchard shelter, not far away from the shelter of Labatut, a similar block, also fallen from the roof, bears traces of two red bovids outlined in black. The blocks in the Labatut shelter were buried between two Perigordian levels (IV and V), whereas the block in the Blanchard shelter lay on the Aurig-

Fig. 4. Magdalenian V. Engravings, cave of Teyjat. Lengths
1 ft 8 in. and 1 ft. 10 in.

nacian level. The similar techniques indicate a certain contemporaneity and, although theoretically these works could
be of much earlier date, it is probable, since nothing analogous
has been found in earlier levels, that they belong approximately to Perigordian IV.

The finely engraved figures on the blocks found in the
Teyjat cave (Fig. 4) can confidently be dated to the Magdalenian period. Some of the blocks were buried below a layer
of Magdalenian V which underlay a Magdalenian VI layer;
but, as the levels of the cave are, on the whole, late Magdalenian it may be inferred that the engravings most probably date
from the beginning of the late Magdalenian. This dating is
confirmed by similarities to the *art mobilier* of the same period,
and by the fact that where there are superimposed designs in
caves, engravings similar in style to those of Teyjat are among
the most recent.

This is the only stratigraphic evidence available for the dating of Franco-Cantabrian art. It is scanty, but a study of the
various styles enables us to add a few details. In principle, when
representations on the walls of a cave are exactly similar to
those on the decorated bones and fragments of ivory found in
the archaeological levels, it may be inferred that they all belong to the same period, or even that they are all the work of
the same artist. If the examples of *art mobilier* can be accurately

dated, then so too can the wall art of the same cave. Such absolute similarities seldom occur, however, because the wall paintings and the examples of *art mobilier* were created by different artists, or because they were not created for the same purpose, or because fundamental similarities are often obscured by differences of material, size, and technique. Moreover, cave sanctuaries were rarely used as dwellings, and therefore comparisons have to be made between sites which are relatively distant from each other.

But such close resemblances do occasionally occur. For example, the finely engraved hinds' heads in the Altamira gallery are exact replicas of those engraved on the scapulae found lying in the Solutrean level at the entrance (Fig. 5). This find constituted a chronological landmark in the study of cave art, and it is made even more interesting by the fact that almost identical hinds' heads were found in the early Magdalenian level at Castillo. It would appear, therefore, that in the Cantabrian region similar art existed at the end of the Solutrean and the beginning of the Magdalenian epochs. At Hornos de la Peña a horse engraved on a stalagmite at the cave entrance is almost exactly like an engraving discovered during excavations in the Aurignacian level, and a few flat pieces of schist engraved with silhouettes very similar to those on the walls of the halls were found in the Perigordian hearth of the original entrance to the cave of Gargas in the Pyrenees. It has therefore been concluded that the two sets of engravings are late Perigordian.

These meagre data provide no more than clues. Added to a more exact knowledge of the stages of development of *art mobilier*, however, they have enabled the various styles of cave art to be studied in terms of their chronological evolution. As far as the portrayal of animals is concerned, there is fairly consistent evidence that Aurignacian and Perigordian treatment of the perspective of legs and horns was very different from that of the Magdalenian. In the Magdalenian, the period of the

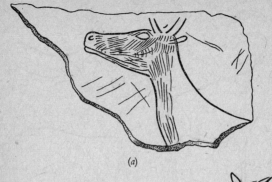

(a)

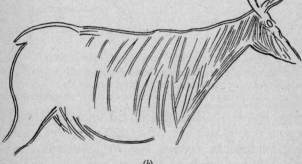

(b)

Fig. 5. (a) Doe's head engraved on a fragment of shoulder blade, Altamira, Solutrean.

(b) Doe engraved on a wall between the Hall of polychrome paintings and the galleries beyond. Length 2 ft 5 in.

The contemporaneity of the two works is apparent.

highest achievement of prehistoric art, animals were portrayed in normal perspective – that is to say, one leg of a pair was shown covering part of the other, and two antlers, or two horns were depicted with one partially covered by the other (Fig. 6c). The Perigordian artists, on the contrary, used the style named by Abbé Breuil 'twisted perspective'. Instead of portraying what they actually saw, they showed unseen details which they knew existed and thus substituted a mental for

Fig. 6. Different types of perspective in Palaeolithic art.
(a) Ibex at Pair-non-Pair with extremities in absolute profile.
(b) Cervid at Lascaux with antlers in 'twisted perspective'.
(c) Magdalenian bison at Teyjat with horns, legs, and hoofs in true perspective.

a visual realism. Children often do this when they draw, and show the four wheels of a car or the two eyes of a human being, for example, in profile. The Perigordian artists showed the body in profile with a frontal view of the head and legs in order to avoid the difficulty of depicting legs, horns, antlers, or ears on two planes (Fig. 6b). This style, characteristic of the animal figures of the Perigordian period, is also fairly common in other primitive forms of animal art.★ Less is known of the cruder Aurignacian style, partly because traces of it are not so common, and partly because some of the representations formerly attributed to this culture are now considered to be Perigordian. This has led to some confusion. The characteristic of the Aurignacian style is the rendering of animal figures in absolute profile with only one leg, one horn, one ear, or one

★ Striking examples of 'twisted perspective' are to be found in portrayals of stags in medieval illuminated manuscripts, in Polish folk art, in Chinese art, and in contemporary children's drawings. Examples could be cited *ad infinitum*.

antler of a pair showing (Fig. 6a). There are exceptions to this however: the horns or the antlers are sometimes represented in 'twisted perspective' and the legs omitted or barely indicated. Exceptional rigidity and lack of movement are also characteristics of the Aurignacian style.

These few general rules are commonly used to classify isolated examples of cave art for which there is no other guide. They may be taken as valid on the whole provided that their application is not too rigid and is linked to an appreciation of the general character of the work, which can be gained only by long study in the cave itself. It must be emphasized that characteristics considered to be Perigordian are frequently present in examples of Magdalenian art, and Magdalenian characteristics are often found in examples of Perigordian art. Numerous instances can be cited. For example, the polychrome bison at Altamira with hoofs in 'twisted perspective' are considered to belong to a very evolved Magdalenian art, whereas the black bulls at Lascaux (Plates 1 and 18), whose hindquarters show a very skilful use of perspective, but whose hoofs are in 'twisted perspective', are attributed to the Perigordian era. Similarly, the absolute profile concept is not confined to Aurignacian art: there are figures in this style on a Perigordian pebble at La Colombière (Ain); and the bison of the Grotte de la Grèze, which is attributed to Solutrean art, is depicted in like manner. The cultures to which these styles belong are not to be determined by a rigid application of semi-mathematical rules, but rather by a careful examination of all accumulated evidence, both documentary and circumstantial.

THE SUPERPOSITIONS

Frequently, for reasons not yet known, several designs and figures were painted or engraved one on top of the other on the same surface without the earlier one being first rubbed off. It is clear that when two (or more) designs have been thus superposed, the earlier will be covered by the more recent. From this it follows in an indirect way that the stratigraphic method used for the study of layers on the site may also be applied to the study of superpositions.

Sculptures provide very few examples of superpositions, whereas superpositions are frequent on paintings and engravings in almost all decorated caves, including Lascaux. They serve to establish the various stages of cave art only when similar characteristics are found superposed in like order in several caves, or in several parts of the same cave.

When an engraving and a painting are superposed one upon the other, it is easy to detect which of them is the earlier by noting whether the paint is scratched off by the engraved line or the engraving obscured by the colouring material. When two paintings are superposed, even though the underlying layer of paint may be thicker, better preserved, of fresher appearance and therefore more clearly visible than the more recent layer, which may have faded or flaked, a careful examination will seldom fail to establish the chronological sequence of the two layers.

The deciphering of two superposed engravings is a more difficult task, although in certain instances a study of the intersections of the engraved lines may establish which of them is the earlier. However, even when no superpositions are present, an examination of the relative positions of two representations may sometimes reveal which of them is the earlier; or, in the case of a composite design, which part is the most recent. On a large panel in the cave of Pech-Merle, for example, there are two horses surrounded by several hands encircled with black (Plate 38). It is quite evident that the hands are of later date than the horses, since it is difficult to imagine how the artist could have managed to distribute them in such a way as to leave the exact space necessary for the two large horses in the centre. At Lascaux too it is evident that the head and shoulders of an incomplete horse were painted after the two bulls' heads on either side of it (Plate 1); the artist clearly refrained from completing the horse in order to avoid disfiguring the bulls' horns.

If the superpositions in a cave follow a regular sequence and if a certain style or technique is always found underlying another style or technique, particularly if superpositions in other caves follow a like sequence, the inference is that the phenomenon is general and a ruling valid for the particular region in question may be accepted. For example, the polychrome paintings in the Valley of the Vézère (Font-de-Gaume) and those in the Cantabrian Pyrénees (Altamira) were found to be superposed on line paintings or paintings in flat wash. It has been concluded, therefore, that polychrome paintings marked the last stage in the flowering of Magdalenian art. Similar superposed sequences have been established elsewhere, and details of these will be given later.

From 1934 onwards Abbé Breuil * was able to establish the broad stages of cave art by the use of these various chronological guides. He states that there were two more or less independent cycles of development – first, an Aurignacio-Perigordian cycle, then a Solutreo-Magdalenian cycle.

BREUIL'S AURIGNACIO-PERIGORDIAN CYCLE

The artists of this cycle began by tracing sinuous lines on the clay surface of certain cave walls with the fingers or by means of toothed implements. The meandering trails appear to have been made aimlessly at first, but later they were used to form rudimentary animal silhouettes. These 'macaronis', as they are called, are found at Arcy-sur-Cure, Cabrerets, Gargas, etc. Hands stencilled in red, black, or yellow have likewise been found in the numerous caves belonging to this first cycle – for example, Cabrerets, Gargas, Castillo, etc. – and

---

* H. Breuil, *Congrès préhistorique de France, 1934.* The theories put forward in this paper have been slightly modified by fresh finds – particularly the discovery of Lascaux (cf. *Four Hundred Centuries of Cave Art*, pp. 38–40).

they are of very early date. In addition to stencilled hands, animal silhouettes in yellow, red, and sometimes black outline represent the earliest form of painting on cave walls. Such silhouettes have been found at Lascaux, though there they are almost entirely effaced or painted over with more recent figures; at Pech-Merle, at Font-de-Gaume – where the rhinoceros painted in the last narrow passage is an interesting example – and at Castillo, etc. At a later stage the Perigordian artists began to fill in the silhouettes with a wash which was generally a uniform black or red; the contours became larger and the lines broader. Sometimes the artist produced a striking effect of relief by leaving some part or parts of the figures uncoloured, or by varying the density of the colour. Many of the paintings at Lascaux, the small black bovids at Font-de-Gaume, several of the figures at Cabrerets, and most of those at Le Portel belong to this developed style of Perigordian art. The bichrome animals and the animals filled in entirely in black at Lascaux would seem to mark both the peak and the final stage of the Aurignacio-Perigordian cycle.

Whereas engraving developed simultaneously with painting, no wall sculptures are known which can be dated to the beginning of the Aurignacio-Perigordian cycle. The earliest engravings are of animal silhouettes in absolute profile and very stiff in style, such as those at Pair-non-Pair, a great part of those in the caves of Gabillou near Musidans in the Dordogne, and the figures at Ebbou in Les Gorges of the Ardèche which were discovered in 1946. Later, the silhouettes became less rigid and more natural. Horns were shown in 'twisted perspective' for a longer time than legs. The greater part of the engravings at Lascaux belong to this period.

BREUIL'S SOLUTREO-MAGDALENIAN CYCLE

The first Solutreans to appear in South-western Europe towards the end of the Perigordian cycle were not artists: no work of art has ever been found in the earliest sites of this culture. The magnificent 'laurel-leaf' blades (or bi-facial foliates) with elongated points belong to this intermediate Solutrean cycle, but, like 'willow-leaf' blades, shouldered 'willow-leaf' points and the first engravings on stone, they are found only in the latest levels. These Solutrean engravings have been found at Badegoule (Dordogne), Champs-Blancs (Dordogne), the cave of Parpallo near Valencia in Spain, etc., and in various Perigordian and Solutrean levels of these sites, painted and engraved figures – mainly of animals – have been found on stone plaques. It is a remarkable fact that whereas the Solutrean industry is distinguished from the industries of the Perigordian and Magdalenian period by the extreme elegance of its flint working and the poverty of its bone tools, the art of this period does not reveal any distinctly characteristic style. Engravings are poor in quality and, though it has been clearly established that the Solutreans used pigments, since traces of these have been found in their occupation levels, no wall-paintings which can be dated with certainty to the Solutrean period are known. Traces of black paint (probably representing one animal in pursuit of another) found on a limestone block at the Solutrean site of Fourneau du Diable merely prove that very large paintings on stone existed at that period, and nothing is known of the style or technique.

On the other hand the Solutrean era was an age of sculpture. The frieze of Le Roc (Charente) and the bovids of Fourneau du Diable at Bourdeilles belong to this period. Other sculpture of the same style, such as that at the Poisson Shelter, which dates from the late Perigordian, or the frieze of sculptured horses at Cap Blanc and the frieze at Angles-sur-Anglin dating from the early Magdalenian, has also been found. There is therefore no clear picture of the artistic evolution of the period marking the end of the Perigordian and the beginning of the Magdalenian within which flourished a Solutrean art, the best examples of which are considered to be the sculptures of the Vallée du Roc.

Apart from the intermediate Solutrean period, the second phase of Palaeolithic art dates from the Magdalenian era. At the end of the Solutrean the flint industries began to deteriorate and the bone industry to develop anew. These tendencies increased at the beginning of the Magdalenian, when the inferior flint working contrasted sharply with the excellence of the bone industry which came to full flower in phases IV, V, VI of this culture. In the main, the first examples of *art mobilier* were very fine sculptures on bone and ivory and engravings on cut bone silhouettes. The art of engraving, which reached its zenith in the middle and late Magdalenian, was practised on stone as well as bone however and often attained great beauty. No painting has yet been found on any Magdalenian *art mobilier*.

Nevertheless, sites of the Magdalenian period contain larger quantities of pigments than are found on sites of earlier cultures. Flat pebbles and thin pieces of schist, which were probably used to crush and thin the ochre, have been found, still stained with colour, on sites of this period. The earliest wall-paintings of the cycle consist of very simple designs in black line; later, the outlines broadened and, like those of the preceding cycle, were gradually filled in until they developed finally into modelled figures of great beauty, such as the black figures at Niaux. The last phase of Magdalenian cave art is represented by the magnificent polychrome figures at Font-de-Gaume in the Dordogne and Altamira in the Cantabrian Pyrenees. In the course of this artistic development the 'twisted perspective' gradually disappeared, and it is very seldom found in the polychromes of the best period. After reaching its peak, however, Magdalenian art rapidly became stylized, until finally, apart from the strange, spotted bison of Marsoulas, it degenerated into purely symbolic or decorative designs. Paintings and engravings of the Magdalenian epoch are generally found together in the same cave; sometimes the engravings are placed alongside the paintings, and sometimes

TABLE 2

COMPARISON OF PAINTINGS OF THE
AURIGNACIO-PERIGORDIAN CYCLE WITH THOSE OF THE
SOLUTREO-MAGDALENIAN CYCLE

This simplified table is puzzling in that it shows recurring similarities which suggest contemporaneity, whereas a study of the styles, particularly the perspective of horns and hoofs, indicates two independent cycles. It also shows that the Aurignacio-Perigordian cycle is yellow and red and the Solutreo-Magdalenian cycle black. Only a complete inventory of all examples corresponding to each stage shown on this table could provide a solution of these problems.

Aurignacio-Perigordian Cycle	*Solutreo-Magdalenian Cycle*
Uniform brown figures	Polychrome figures
	Figures in brown colour
	Figures filled in with spots
	Figures in black shaded relief
Figures in black outline	Figures in thin black line
Bi-chrome figures	
Figures in red or black flat wash, first incomplete, then complete	Figures in flat black wash
Figures in broad, blurred bands	Figures in blurred black bands
Line designs in yellow, red, and sometimes black	Very simple black line designs
Large red animals in primitive style	Large red symbols. Red or yellow meanders
Hands encircled with colour. Hand imprints. Punctuations	

both painting and engraving are used in the execution of one and the same work. The later the period, the finer and more numerous become the engravings; they tend also to decrease in size.

In the foregoing paragraphs an outline has been given of the principal stages of evolution of Palaeolithic art as set forth by Abbé Breuil. Whether they have now been conclusively established or not, only time and fresh discoveries will show.

For the time being, however, they provide the best framework for the known examples of Palaeolithic art – indeed, the only one yet devised.

It is possible that Breuil's classifications could be simplified by a separate study of the sculptures in the open sites of South-western France on the one hand, and those in underground sanctuaries on the other. Although to a certain extent contemporaneous, they were created for different purposes and were probably inspired by different cultural traditions.★ Apart from the Solutrean sculptures, there would seem to be an un-doubted continuity in wall art from the end of the Perigordian to the beginning of the Magdalenian, and indeed it is prob-able that the painting and engraving traditions of the first Breuil cycle still guided these arts in some measure in the second. The proximity in time of these cycles, which followed an immensely long period without any known artistic mani-festations and preceded the Mesolithic and Neolithic cultures of the post-glacial period whose artistic traditions were ex-tremely barren, indicates undeniable affiliation. Although little is known of these, it would not seem impossible one day to establish a continuity between the two cycles and show that one was merely an extension of the other. Lascaux would pro-vide an important link and perhaps prove to be less remote in time from the marvellous polychromes of the finest period than is generally believed.†

★ Cf. A. Laming, *La Signification de l'art rupestre paléolithique*. In the press.
† This is merely a hypothesis and requires careful examination. It is based on two essential facts: (*a*) The existence at Font-de-Gaume and Altamira of examples of Perigordian style underlying the polychromes. Similar super-positions have been found in other caves; so there is evidence of continuity in the use of these caves from one period to the other; (*b*) the parallelism of the phases established by Abbé Breuil for each of the two cycles (cf. *Four Hundred Centuries of Cave Art*, pp. 38–9) as shown in Table 2.

Man's Earliest Sanctuaries

Cave art holds a special place in the cultural history of mankind. It developed entirely within the Upper Palaeolithic, which corresponds approximately to the second half of the last glacial period when *Homo sapiens* made his appearance. The pre-hominids, followed by the hominids, had spread throughout the Old World – Asia, Europe, and Africa – hundreds of thousands of years earlier. They led the primitive lives of nomad hunters, but they had discovered fire and had learned to fashion weapons and tools in stone. They appear to have adapted themselves easily to climatic changes, which in our regions alternated between subarctic conditions and conditions warmer and damper than those prevailing today.

In the last inter-glacial period a new human type emerged – Neanderthal Man. He possessed a more varied range of tools than his predecessors, which implies that he led a more complex life, and he made use of fire not only to provide warmth, but also to cook his food. Now, for the first time in the history of mankind, the dead were buried according to strictly defined rites, which point to certain religious beliefs. It is possible that Neanderthal Man may have painted his body, for traces of bioxide of manganese have been found at certain sites, but no work of art, even of the most rudimentary kind, has ever been found in association with his remains.

After several tens of thousands of years, during which period Neanderthal industries slowly evolved, the climate again grew colder. The Hippopotamus, the *Elephas meridionalis*, and the *Rhinoceros mercki* were gradually replaced by animals physically better adapted to the new conditions – the woolly rhinoceros, the thick-fleeced mammoth, the cave bear, etc. Forests and swamps gave place to steppes and, further north, at the edge of the great continental glacier which now covered the north of Eurasia, to the tundra. Man, who during the warm period had probably lived in huts made of branches, now took refuge in the caves where his accumulated débris has been found.

It was at this period that true *Homo sapiens* made his first appearance. The place of origin of *Homo sapiens* has never been determined: it may have been Western Asia, but this is still uncertain. His descendants appeared in Western Europe in successive waves about the middle of the last glacial period and were already in possession of a characteristic industry very different from the Mousterian industries of Neanderthal Man.

In the caves the remains belonging to these newcomers cover those of the last Neanderthals; but it is not known how this came about or how it happened that the first *Homo sapiens*, inventor of a more complex and better-equipped industry and indubitably of greater intellectual capacity than Neanderthal Man, gradually invaded the territories inhabited by him. No trace of armed conflict between the two human groups has ever been discovered. In any case, the area of habitation must have been very thinly populated, and even if there had been a conflict it would not necessarily have been in the form of an armed clash: there might merely have been skirmishes, individual killings, etc., followed by the progressive retreat of Neanderthal Man to the fringes of a territory less favourable to human habitation.

At all events, *Homo sapiens* was the survivor, and Neanderthal Man rapidly became extinct in Europe. The human beings who replaced him were of a physical type closely resembling present-day Man. They worked flint blades and bone points of new types and their technical methods were spread over a vast area – Europe, the Near East, North Africa. Apart from their industry, however, practically nothing is known of the culture or beliefs of these early Perigordians in Western Europe; and no traces of burials or any artistic achievements attributable to them have ever come to light.

At that time South-western Europe was also invaded by a different cultural group – the Aurignacians, and the contact between the different traditions and beliefs of the two cultures brought about many changes. There was an undoubted improvement in the industries, although it was of slow development: bone, ivory, and stone remained the essential raw materials, and hunting and fishing the fundamental activities for a long time to come. Nevertheless, in another sphere Man took a long stride forward – he conceived Art and created Beauty.

The paintings of the Palaeolithic sanctuaries mark a culminating point in the history of mankind, or perhaps it would be more precise to say that they represent a culminating point for the historian of mankind. On the cultural plane there is no knowledge of what artistic manifestations preceded these paintings – what dances, music, or songs – and there is no knowledge of any beliefs or ceremonies. They are all lost for ever, for without tangible evidence their existence cannot be accepted. Apart from the earliest burials, these Palaeolithic sanctuaries provide the first testimony of any human activity unconnected with immediate material needs. On the emotional plane the paintings seem to bear witness to a sense of religious awe, of harmony, and of beauty which brings these remote ancestors of ours closer to us; on the technical plane to show a capacity to create magnificent works of art; and on the intellectual plane to mark the first step towards conceptual art and writing itself.

The first groping efforts of the Aurignacio-Perigordian artists developed with amazing speed into huge impressive paintings such as those at Lascaux. It was indeed several millennia (exactly how many is not known) before this first school of monumental painting reached the period of its finest achievements; but, in comparison with the hundreds of thousands of years preceding them, these few millennia are insignificant, and the artistic development within this period was so rapid that it can justly be described as a sudden outburst of man's new-found faculties.

Magdalenian art, which represents the culminating stage of this period of artistic achievement, was more subtle, delicate, and varied. The duration of its flowering is unknown, but it may have lasted for some thousands of years. The forms of art so recently invented by man – engraving, sculpture, and painting both on small objects and on huge walls – were gradually developed and perfected during this period, though no fundamental changes took place.

Cave art, however, was but a bright flame which burnt itself out. The Western European cultures which followed the Magdalenian at the end of the last glacial period and the beginning of the post-glacial era have left no evidence of any comparable graphic art. Indeed, there are no traces at all of any such monumental artistic achievements in Western Europe until the renewed flowering of religious art in the Middle Ages produced its magnificent crypts, basilicas, and cathedrals. It is not yet known whether there was a complete disappearance of the genius and skill of the Palaeolithic artist: possibly certain engraved rocks in Scandinavia (Fig. 7) may be directly linked to a Palaeolithic tradition handed down by the last Magdalenians at the extreme end of the glacial period; * and in South-western Europe the painted rocks of Eastern Spain probably belong to the end of the Palaeolithic, but there is no evidence that they are linked in any way to the graphic art of the Mediterranean civilizations. Attempts have sometimes been made to establish a connexion between the engraved slate palettes and the animal-headed gods of the ancient Egyptians and the semi-human figures of the Palaeolithic artists, but there is no positive evidence of any relationship. Moreover, a gap of several millennia separates the last Palaeolithic works of art from the earliest known Egyptian engravings. If there is any affinity, it is more likely to be in the sphere of religious belief than in the sphere of graphic art.

* See H. C. Bandi and J. Malinger, *L'Art préhistorique*, Bâle and Paris, 1952, Part III, 'L'Art Arctique', pp. 143–66 (with bibliography).

Fig. 7. Reindeer engraved on rockface, Norway. Example of animal
art of the prehistoric epoch.

Palaeolithic art, of which the Lascaux paintings are among
the most magnificent examples, thus stands out as an isolated
phenomenon in time, the forerunner of other great artistic
achievements. Neither in human societies nor in nature is
progress constant: each advance is made in sudden leaps and
bounds followed by halts and fresh starts.

CHAPTER I

THE LASCAUX CAVE

The Discovery of the Cave

ON 12 September 1940 four boys from Montignac * in Périgord were strolling along the wooded plateau which domin-
ates the valley of the Vézère from a height of more than 300
ft, when suddenly their dog disappeared down a hole which
had been opened up a few years earlier by the fall of a fir-tree
uprooted in a storm and was now half-concealed by brambles
and brushwood. No one had ever thought of exploring this
hole: indeed, the local peasants had covered it with a pile of
brushwood to prevent their animals from falling into it.

The boys called their dog in vain: they could neither see nor
hear it. When they threw a stone down the hole, it seemed to
be very deep. Nevertheless, one of them forced his way
through the tangle at the cost of a few scratches and lowered
himself into a horizontal fissure of the rock. It was not very
deep, but the floor of damp, slippery clay sloped abruptly
downwards, until, at a depth of about 52 ft, the boy found
himself in a low gallery without a chink of daylight. He was
followed by his companions and soon all four boys and their
dog were reunited. The gallery seemed to lead further into the
gloom, which the matches they lit failed to illuminate; so,
when their supply became exhausted, they had no choice but
to climb up the fissure again and push their way through
the hole to daylight.

There is not a single person in the valley of the Vézère who

* Two of the boys, Ravidat and Marsal, are natives of the Commune and
subsequently became guides to the cave – indeed they still fill this office. The
third, Agnel, was on holiday in Montignac, and the fourth, Coencas, was a
refugee there.

does not know of the painted caves and the rich sites which have been discovered there; and every young Perigordian is something of a prehistorian, for their schoolmasters always allocate a certain amount of time to the study of Prehistory. The four boys were therefore highly excited by their adventure; but they told no one of it. The following day they returned to the hole with a rope and a rough-and-ready lamp which they had contrived from an old grease-gun: the great moment of discovery was at hand. Following the low gallery which they had not been able to explore the previous day, they came to a vast oval chamber whose walls were painted right up to the roof with enormous bulls surrounded by horses and deer. There were also traces of other figures, but their inexperienced eyes could not decipher them.

Two galleries led from the Great Hall: on their walls red, yellow, black, or brown ibexes, horses, massive bulls, smaller cows, and files of deer followed each other in the utmost confusion. Some figures were isolated, others depicted in long files or in jumbled groups; many of them were painted, some were painted and engraved, and others, more difficult to distinguish, engraved only. The four boys were much elated by the discovery they had made, and ran to tell their former schoolmaster, Monsieur Laval, of their experience. At first he was sceptical, but finally he was convinced and accompanied the boys to the cave. What he saw there astounded him, and he lost no time in informing prehistorians that a new painted cave had just been discovered.

Abbé Breuil, the eminent expert on Palaeolithic art, was advised of the discovery on 17 September and arrived on the spot almost immediately. On 21 September, together with Dr Cheynier and Abbé Bouyssonnie, he inspected the cave. All three of them were immediately convinced of the authenticity of the discovery; they declared it to be one of the most beautiful Palaeolithic caves known and stated that the condition of the paintings was remarkable. Monsieur D. Peyrony, at that time Director of Antiquities of the district, and the Prefect of the Dordogne were told of the cave, which they visited in their turn on 27 and 28 September. The news then spread like wild-fire, and the little town of Montignac was soon in a state of great excitement. Everyone wanted to see the cave, and it was not long before large numbers of visitors arrived – journalists, photographers, and sightseers – to whom Abbé Breuil kindly explained the paintings and commented on them. To prevent any damage being done to the cave, the four boys camped near the entrance.

Immediately its discovery was announced, the cave was classified as a historical monument and a plan drawn up for its equipment and protection. But it was war-time; so all that could be done was to close it to the public, who might do damage, and protect it from contact with the outside atmo-sphere, for variations in degrees of temperature and humidity play an important part in the deterioration of Palaeolithic paintings.* Work on the cave was not resumed until 1948, long after the liberation of France. Apart from the fitting-up of the interior, this work included the erection of a stairway to the entrance, the organization of a system to prevent water draining from the plateau into the cave, the construction of two protective walls at the entrance with a waiting-room for visitors between, and finally, the building of a roadway to the cave in place of the old path (Plate 45).

* A great deal has been said about the deterioration of the Lascaux paintings since their discovery, but it would seem that these rumours are unfounded. Specialists are sent there every year to verify the constancy of the colours by means of photographs. No deterioration or change of colour has ever been found from one year to another. However, in order to avoid too great an escape of carbonic acid gas which might engender a deterioration of the paint-ings and cause discomfort to visitors, troughs of lime were installed at several points in the cave to absorb the carbon gas and these troughs are renewed at regular intervals. In addition, the number of visitors has been limited to 500 a day. (It has been estimated that in 1953 there were 30,000 visitors, and from 1 January to 15 September 1954 43,928 visitors were recorded. S.P.F., 1954, p. 488.)

Today Lascaux is one of the most famous sites of Palaeo-lithic rock art in Western Europe, and every year thousands of tourists and dozens of experts visit the cave to admire its paint-ings and engravings. The equipment – stairs, cement paths, electric lighting – has been designed as discreetly as possible and allows the cave to be visited as easily as a museum. Care has likewise been taken to illuminate each painting to the best advantage. All this work was indeed essential if the cave was to attract a large public, who would hardly care to sink into slimy clay or slide about on damp ground by the light of a candle; but those who wish to experience and understand the magic of the cave must try to forget the intrusion of modern man; they must ignore the reflectors and cement paths, the admiring throng and their comments, and envisage Lascaux deserted and mysterious as the four boys found it – exactly as it was fifteen thousand years ago.

The electric lighting, pale and constant, overpowers the paintings, for an important part is played by the irregularities of the rock-face; and the presence of people has the effect of curbing the imagination and robbing the cave of its mystery. It must be visited for a long period in solitude by the flickering light of a small hand-lamp as similar as possible to those used by the Palaeolithic artists – a candle-lamp, for example, for then, in the silence, the sanctuary of the Palaeolithic hunters with its animals leaping and running in the play of the light and shadows is seen unchanged – overwhelming and awe-inspiring.

Description of the Cave

The cave of Lascaux is situated on the left bank of the Vézère about 1½ miles to the south-east of Montignac. It lies within the small estate of Lascaux, the property of the Count and Countess de la Rochefoucauld-Montbel. In Palaeolithic times this district was the centre of a region in the full flower of a highly developed artistic culture – perhaps the first in the history of mankind.

The present entrance – which may have been the one used by the Palaeolithic hunters – was the result of a fall of the limestone rock forming the roof of the cave. No other entrance has been discovered up to the present, but it is possible that there are others which are now blocked up. The collapse of the rock at the present entrance could be of comparatively recent date, and Palaeolithic Man may have entered his sanctuary by a gallery opening into the limestone cliffs some 400 yards away. Attempts to find other entrances have produced no results, however, and the clearing of a tunnel has been postponed owing to the difficulty of disposing of the clay blocking. At another place, the entrance to a chamber was revealed, but this chamber does not seem to have been used by Palaeolithic Man, and no further work was undertaken in it on account of the danger of a fall of rock and because no discovery of any interest could be anticipated from its continuance.

The problem of the entrance thus remains unsolved. The distribution of the engraved signs suggests that it might have lain beyond the network of narrow tunnels and pits extending from the Chamber of Felines. Numerous signs, including some of the quadrilaterals so typical of Lascaux, are engraved there, and it is an interesting fact that at Font-de-Gaume the first designs in the cave are a series of signs placed at the entrance to a passage of difficult ascent.

The interior of the cave has at least two levels. The upper level contains the Palaeolithic works of art, the lower level or levels are inaccessible and were probably equally impenetrable in the time of the reindeer-hunters, but the 'suction pits' found at certain points of the cave and the dull sound made at others by striking the ground with the foot bear witness to their existence. At two points vertical gullies make it possible to reach cavities on a lower level than the rest of the cave which have outlets blocked up by sand or clay. One of these gullies is situated beyond the Chamber of Felines, the other forms the Shaft of the Dead Man. The furthermost end of the Main Gallery is also lower than the rest of the cave.

In periods of rain, before the cave was equipped as now, water draining from the plateau used to penetrate the crevice at the entrance,* flow down the slope, and trickle out into the Great Hall of the Bulls, where it eventually formed and filled a series of large saucer-like hollows rimmed with calcite which lie on the ground like a chain of fountain basins. At the time of the discovery, the ground, untrodden for thousands of years, was carpeted with calcite of dazzling whiteness. Towards the end of the Hall a funnel-shaped depression formed a 'suction pit' through which water coming from outside the cave flowed down to the lower levels. In order to drain the Hall, the saucer-like hollows, which contained vast quantities of water, were pierced and thousands of gallons of water rushed down into the funnel which was partly blocked. This sudden torrent washed away the masses of loose earth lodged in its base, and must have caused considerable disturbance in the lower galleries, for the next day there were falls of earth which in some places reached a height of well over 3 ft. According to Abbé Breuil,† there may have been other such falls in the cave since the end of the Palaeolithic; the floor level of the Main Gallery may once have been higher than it is now, and the paintings, which today are seen at a height of several feet, within arms' length of the artists working on them.

There has certainly been very little alteration in the floor level of the Painted Gallery, however, since Palaeolithic times, for the three red animals at the far end, considered to be the oldest figures in the cave, are painted at the present ground level. Indeed the floor of this part of the cave is more likely to have become raised than lowered, and it is possible that the

---

* H. Breuil, 'Lascaux', *S.P.F.*, Nos. 6, 7, 8 (June, July, August) 1950, pp. 354–65.

† *Op. cit.*, p. 356.

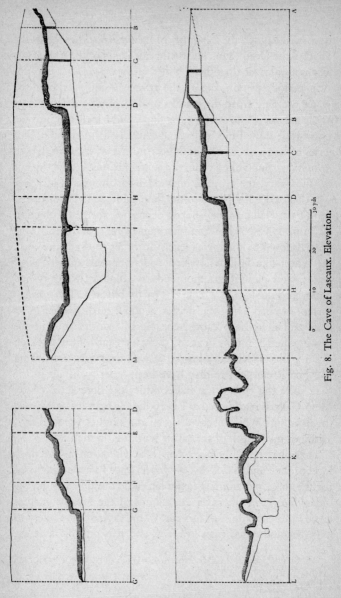

Fig. 8. The Cave of Lascaux. Elevation.

60

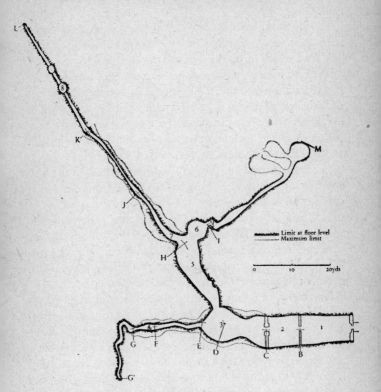

Fig. 9. The Cave of Lascaux. Plan.

1. and 2. Entrance Hall and staircase leading into cave.
   3. The Great Hall of the Bulls.
   4. The Painted Gallery, ending in a tunnel G–G[1].
   5. The Lateral Passage.
   6. The Chamber of Engravings.
   7. The Main Gallery.
   8. The Chamber of Felines.
   9. The Shaft of the Dead Man and its extension.

narrow terminal tunnel may once have been accessible to man.

The limestone mass out of which the cave is hollowed is not homogeneous: it is divided into two almost horizontal levels.* The level which forms the roof and the upper part of the walls of the cave is non-porous, fissures in it are rare, and there are no stalactite formations; the surface is smooth and in two of the principal chambers is covered with a thin, even coating of dazzlingly white calcite crystals. This coating is older than the paintings and its formation ceased after they were executed. Calcite efflorescences are rarely found on a painting.

In certain places large pieces of rock have flaked off the wall and fallen to the floor. Some fell before and some after the completion of the paintings, for a few still bear a coating of calcite, and others traces of paint. No further calcite deposit formed after their fall and their places on the wall are marked by large irregular patches of a yellowish colour which the Palaeolithic artists often used to form the outlines of the backs, necks, or hindquarters of the animals they were depicting.†

The lower limestone layer is separated from the upper by a regular almost horizontal ledge which is clearly visible. Erosion here has been less rapid than elsewhere, and the ledge forms a cornice around the chambers varying in width from a few inches to more than a yard. The surface is corrugated and covered with rounded bosses; with few exceptions it has been neither engraved nor painted, and bears no trace of calcite deposit. This straight dark ledge around the chambers and galleries was utilized by the Palaeolithic artists as a ground-line for their paintings, and even, in one instance, as a water-line. (Cf. Plate 33 for the water-line, Plate 1 and the majority of the photographs of the cave for the ground-line.)

* *Op. cit.*, p. 357.
† The flakings are plainly visible on several photographs, e.g. on the neck of the bull of Plate 6 and in the middle of the bovids of Plates 7 and 9. The head of the small deer in the centre top of Plate 4 is entirely formed by one of these natural flakings.

For the most part this cornice is very dark in colour – reddish or almost black, and, when clay-filled depressions are found in its surface, the clay surface is likewise coloured. According to some authorities, this coloration, which is found on horizontal or slanting surfaces, is caused by a fungus growth; others believe that the pigments on the walls flaked very slowly in the perfectly still atmosphere and fell in a fine powder on to the horizontal surfaces. Similar deposits of pigment have been found in other Palaeolithic painted caves such as Les Combarelles or La Mouthe.*

The Paintings and Engravings

Beyond the long slope, of which the first part bears no trace of any work of art and is now converted into a waiting-room, lie the decorated chambers. They can be divided into two main groups – chambers containing paintings only, and chambers containing paintings and engravings as well as a number of designs combining both painting and engraving. In addition to the works in these chambers, there is one extraordinary scene painted at the base of a vertical shaft several feet deep which resembles no other painting in this or any other cave. Apart from these chambers, there is also a gallery about 8 yards wide by 8 feet high, which leads off in a westerly direction close to the entrance of the Great Hall. It was found to be extremely damp and covered with decomposed stalagmite concretions and to contain no trace of painting or engraving. About 12 yards from the entrance it was blocked by a large mass of débris and was therefore condemned as unsafe and sealed up.

* Rivière once had a chemical analysis made of pigments found in similar conditions in the cave of La Mouthe. *L'Homme préhistorique*, March 1903, p. 84. No such analysis has been carried out at Lascaux.

THE GREAT HALL OF THE BULLS

The group of painted chambers consists of the large Hall at the entrance called the Great Hall of the Bulls and a narrow gallery leading off it. The roofs of both are even and more or less regular; but, as the floor slopes down from the entrance to the far end of the gallery, they become increasingly lofty. Above the continuous irregular limestone cornice, the walls and roofs are almost entirely covered by a film of white calcite crystals on which the paintings have been wonderfully preserved.

The Great Hall of the Bulls (Plate 1) is oval in shape; it is about 17 yards long by about 10 yards wide. When it was entered for the first time nearly sixteen years ago, a series of linked saucer-like hollows on different levels patterned the floor with their immaculate whiteness. These hollows were formed by the water which drained from the plateau and penetrated the cave after Palaeolithic Man had abandoned it, as the few traces of human presence found under the calcite deposit prove.

The calcite crystals of the walls appear to have been formed by very slow exudation from the rock, and not deposited drop by drop like stalactites. Little by little this exudation has coated the limestone roof with an extremely hard crust and given it a varnished appearance. On this surface the paintings have been preserved in perfect condition, and the few flakings in no way impair their freshness. Some of the flakings are earlier than the paintings, and the paint has been applied directly on to the limestone; later flakings have left a gap in the paintings. It may be that when flaking occurred after a painting had been executed and while the cave was still used by Palaeolithic Man, the gap was subsequently filled by another painting. For example, the foreleg of the large red-and-black horse of Plate 3 is painted on a flaked patch which must previously have been occupied by the shoulder of a large black bull.

The dimensions and composition of the figures in the Great Hall of the Bulls, and indeed of all the figures in the cave, are exceptional in Palaeolithic art. Four immense black bulls (the largest is about 18 ft long) form a frieze which occupies the major part of the walls at the end of the Hall. Three of them are shown in Indian file, the fourth faces them. They are drawn in thick black line, and a partial filling-in of the legs, thighs, bellies, chests, and muzzles gives a striking effect of relief; other parts of the bodies are speckled with black. Traces of the rough sketches of at least three other bulls, one of them red and very incomplete, are discernible at both ends of the frieze.

On entering the Hall, attention is immediately focused on the black bulls, for the other animals are more modest in size. They consist of bovids, horses, deer, a small bear, and an extraordinary animal which was certainly never part of the actual fauna of Palaeolithic times and which has been most inappropriately named 'The Unicorn'. These animals are scattered all over the walls in apparent confusion.

The first figure to the left of the entrance of the Great Hall is the small head of a horse without any body or legs. The line of its back is traced in red ochre, and the head and the rather blurred mane are black. The body colour is bistre – perhaps because the rock-face at that point is darker in colour. Slightly beyond it the strange so-called Unicorn (Plate 2) appears to be walking towards the interior of the cave. It has massive hindquarters, a sagging belly of conical shape, an almost square muzzle, and, projecting from its forehead, two long, straight horns. The style of the painting is similar to that of the large bulls – contour in thick black line, legs, thighs, and muzzle filled in. The body is marked with large black oval patches. The style seems less skilful than that of the other figures in the Hall, and the movement is stiffer. Although he was so skilful in representing animals that he knew and had studied, the artist was apparently unable to depict an imaginary or mythical animal with equal mastery. Within the hindquarters of this animal the incomplete outline of a small horse is drawn in thin red line, and in the neighbourhood of the shoulder there is a red mark which seems to be the vestige of an earlier animal now almost completely effaced.

In front of the imaginary animal there is a frieze of small black horses all galloping in the same direction. The technique used in the portrayal of these animals is very different from that used for the Unicorn; they are filled in with flat black or blackish wash and vaguely dappled. This frieze was painted later than the Unicorn, for the Unicorn's chest is partly covered by the hindquarters of one of the horses, and its foreleg is outlined by this horse's tail. Where the head of the horse should be there is a large light-coloured space caused by the fall of a rock flake, for a fragment of rock bearing the intact head of the horse was found at the foot of the wall. The fall of this flake also damaged a large black bull, and only the region of its ears, the tip of its muzzle, and the occasional outline of its back remain.

The frieze of black horses consists of six animals, the last of which is very incomplete. They are superposed on the legs and belly of the first of the large intact black bulls and are of later date than the long red horse with black mane which is painted on the bull's flank. This red-and-black horse (Plate 3) appears to have been executed piecemeal. At first sight the legs, mane, and black head seem to have been added to an earlier red animal, but in fact the figure is more complicated. By a good light it is comparatively easy to see that there are in fact two heads – one red, one black – which are more or less parallel to each other. It is even more curious that each of the forelegs has been used to outline the head of another horse with an eye represented by a small black spot and a mane by a series of black hatchings.*

The next group consists of five somewhat stiffly drawn

* These heads have been deciphered by Abbé Glory who has been entrusted by the Ministère des Beaux Arts with the task of compiling a complete inventory of the paintings and engravings of the cave.

small deer scattered between the two bulls which are facing each other (Plate 4). Three of them are a reddish colour, one is bistre, and the last, of which only the antlers are shown, is black. One of them is in superposition with the leg of a bull, but it is difficult to tell which of the figures underlies the other. The colours have become merged; in some places the red of the deer appears to cover the black of the bull, but the order of the superposition is uncertain. A double flaking of the rock in the shape of a fan has been utilized for the antlers of one of the small deer, and the body and head of another are likewise formed by a rock flake. A few strokes have been added to perfect these natural markings, and, though under a strong light they appear to be mere vestiges, in a judiciously placed dimmer light the body and antlers of the small deer stand out clearly. Above the deer, immediately between the horns of the two bulls, there is a fine profiled outline of the head and shoulders of a horse with a reddish body and a blurred black mane (Plate 1). The line of its back is strongly emphasized by a deep natural depression of the rock.

Further on, at the same level as the frieze of black horses and the small deer, three red bovids can be distinguished within the bellies of the two large bulls, their legs resting on the dark cornice. They are painted in flat wash, but their outlines are very indistinct and appear to be faded. In certain places the red of these bovids seems to overlie the black of the bulls, in others it appears to lie under it. The chronological sequence of these figures is as uncertain as that of the small deer, and a mere examination of these paintings is insufficient to establish which of the two series is the earlier. The first of the red bovids is facing the end of the Hall, its massive head lowered as though it were grazing (Fig. 9). It is partially hidden by the genital organs of the bull and is difficult to distinguish. Its hindquarters are outlined by a horizontal protuberance of the rock, and when viewed in a slanting light the flank and bony rump stand out in remarkable relief.

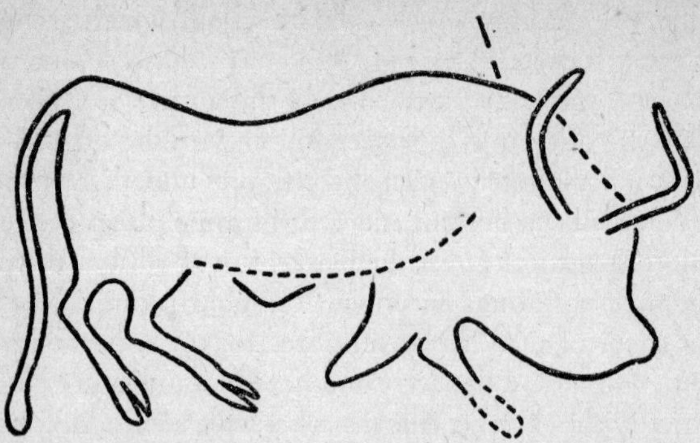

Fig. 10. Red bovid in the Great Hall of the Bulls. The parts shown
in dotted line are masked by, or intermingled with, the contours of
a black bull. Length 8 ft. See Plate 1.

The chest of the bull next to it is crossed by a very small
deer, and its broad belly-line half conceals a small black bear
with upraised snout (Plate 7) whose head, ears, and dorsal
hump are formed by a natural projection of the rock. The
mass of its body is painted in a somewhat darker black perhaps than that of the bull, and it is difficult to distinguish one
body from the other. Only the rump and the head of the bear
protrude above the black band, and below it protrude the
claws, which have been retouched in a very intense black.
This figure is composed of natural bosses and a few touches of
paint, and so is not immediately apparent, but it is a charming and most successful representation. In front of the bear,
and still on a level with the bellies of the bulls, there are two
blurred red masses representing a cow followed by her calf
(Fig. 10). Under the calf there is an isolated pair of red legs
which seems to belong to another small creature whose head
and two ears can be distinguished. A few other barely discernible vestiges, including the incomplete sketch of a large bull,
are of minor importance.

The inventory of the figures in the Great Hall comprises seven large bulls, three other bovids (perhaps four) of slighter build, nine horses, and the vestiges or blurred shapes of at least two others, six deer, one bear, and one mythical animal; it also includes one or two signs (considerably fewer than those in the other chambers), and a dart piercing the nostrils of one of the bulls (Plate 6). In the majority of Palaeolithic caves it is difficult to know if the figures are to be studied individually or in groups of the same species; or if, on the other hand, the paintings on a wall form an ensemble which is to be interpreted as a whole. At Lascaux the careful composition of some groups at least – for example, the black bulls or the galloping horses – is very evident and there is no justification for segregating one animal from another. The determination of the relationship between the different groups is, however, more difficult. Do the juxtapositions merely correspond to different times and purposes? Have the superpositions, on the contrary, a definite purpose? Again a mere examination of the paintings cannot provide satisfactory answers to these questions.

Nevertheless, there is no doubt that the confusion is only

Fig. 11. Red bovid in the Great Hall of the Bulls. The parts shown in dotted line are masked by the black of a bull and are difficult to distinguish. The horns shown in dotted line are black. The small red animal to the left is probably a calf following its mother; below it there is probably another small figure. Length 7 ft 8 in.

apparent. Even where the artists have superposed representations over others of different times, they have tried to retain a certain degree of harmony in the ensemble. This is most evident in the way the head and shoulders of the bichrome horse is framed between the horns of the two gigantic bulls (Plate 1).

There are several reasons why the planned composition of wall art has rarely been considered. The Palaeolithic works of art of the early discoveries often contained a confused medley of figures, and it is this feature of cave art, so foreign to our conception of pictorial composition, which has always been especially noticed and stressed. In addition, unlike any schools of art known to us, the Palaeolithic artists had to make use of natural irregular surfaces which never, or seldom, provided them with a large smooth base for their compositions. The reproduction of these paintings and engravings on paper by hand copies or by photography involves inescapable difficulties: the figures become elongated, distorted, and stretched in every direction, and it is often necessary to isolate a figure from the group to which it belongs before it can be reproduced because the surface on which it is executed is either concave, convex, or very uneven. Sometimes even a photograph can reproduce only a detail of a figure. Gradually, when studying Palaeolithic art, the habit of concentrating on the details of a particular work is formed and the composition is not considered as a whole. Composed ensembles are particularly noticeable at Lascaux, but they exist in nearly all painted caves, and it is essential to try to recognize the place they must have held in the minds of the artists who created them.

THE PAINTED GALLERY

In the Painted Gallery the coating of calcite is thicker and more continuous than that in the Great Hall of the Bulls. The deposit continued to form after the execution of the paintings, especially towards the far end of the Gallery, where certain figures are lightly veiled by a white efflorescence. The flaking of the walls has been very slight and is everywhere of earlier date than the paintings. No rock flakes have been found on the floor.

The length of the gallery is about 22 yards and the width at floor level about 2½ yards at most. The space between the two dark and irregular limestone cornices is very narrow, but about midway between floor and ceiling the gallery widens and the walls become smoother and much lighter in colour because of the coating of white calcite. This surface is richly painted. The cornices are an extension of those in the Great Hall of the Bulls and are more or less horizontal, but, since the floor slopes downwards towards the end of the Gallery, the visitor sees the paintings at a higher and higher level the further he moves forward. At the farthermost end the calcite crystals cover the entire wall and the whole of one large painted panel extends from floor to ceiling.

The paintings in the Gallery contain more clearly defined groups than those in the Great Hall; one or two animals are shown isolated and unconnected with others, but most of the figures form deliberately composed groups or friezes.

The right-hand wall is more richly painted than the left. The forelegs of one of the bulls of the Great Hall extend into the Gallery, and the first figure below them is a small nigger-brown horse with a very elongated head and a body in a poor state of preservation. It has three forelegs, either because the artist intended to complete the figure later or because he intended thereby to represent an animal in movement. There are similar examples of the addition of a leg or of pairs of legs in other Palaeolithic caves (Fig. 12).

Above the three-legged horse, a deer (Plate 11) with large antlers turns its head towards the interior of the Gallery; only its back, chest, and head are shown, and they are filled in with short, blurred parallel strokes, but the thin black line which the

Fig. 12. Multi-legged animals in Palaeolithic art.

(a) Wild boar at Altamira.

(b) Horse at Lascaux. This figure is in a poor state of preservation. There are probably two outlines of the chest.

artist used to sketch in the outline can still be distinguished. On its back there is an ochre-coloured line, and beneath the figure a row of thirteen large black dots. In front of it a quadrilateral has been drawn in a fine black line; such quadrilaterals and more complicated versions of them are one of the mysteries of Lascaux. Besides these figures, the back and neck of a small black horse are visible on this panel.

The group which follows is the most outstanding in the cave on account of the boldness of its execution. It is composed of horses and bovids painted on both the wall and the roof (Plate 7). The horses are painted in bistre and black (Plate 10), the bovids in red and black (Plate 9). Large white spaces which give an effect of relief have been left in the interior of some of the figures and probably represent the various markings on their coats. One of the horses clearly underlies a bovid, on which the leg of another seems to be superposed, but this may be due to retouching. Darts in flight are shown between several of the figures in this group. A line pierces the chest of one of the large bovids which is painted in red with part of its body left white. Its forelegs are placed on the left-hand cornice, the whole of its body follows the arch of the roof, and the lines of its croup and tail are lost in the right-hand cornice. The composition and execution of this painting are remarkable, and the whole effect is extremely striking. The group covers an entire section of the Gallery – both the right- and the left-hand walls as well as the roof. It consists in all of three red and black bovids, six bistre or bistre and black horses, and one incomplete black horse.

Farther along the right-hand wall there is a very complex frieze (Plate 12). Its central figure is a large cow with its forelegs extended, and its hindlegs bent under it as though it were leaping over the large latticed sign in front of it. The cow is black on a barely visible red ground; the latticed sign is red. Below the cow, which is facing the far end of the Gallery, there is a charming frieze consisting of five small horses with stiff legs and blurred manes. These horses – red and black, bistre and black, or completely black – are facing the opposite way, towards the Great Hall of the Bulls. The smallest horse is painted in red and black and resembles a child's wooden toy. There are no true bichromes among these figures: in each case the two shades seem to have been evenly blended, as if black paint had been applied over a first ground of a lighter colour. Above the cow a bull's head outlined in black recalls the bulls of the Great Hall, and does not seem to be related in any way to the ensemble of this panel.

Below the large latticed sign in front of the cow an almost shapeless bistre silhouette encircled with black is distinguishable. It is probably a horse. It is followed by a further series of horses in tones of bistre, black, and particularly red, arranged in two facing groups. They are somewhat crude in style and in a poor state of preservation. The frieze ends with two ibexes confronting each other but separated by a latticed sign similar to that painted in front of the leaping cow. The silhouettes of these two long-horned ibexes are rendered in a series of punctuations. Under the second ibex the outlines of two small incomplete horses are still decipherable. In its entirety the panel consists of a bovid, two ibexes, and seventeen horses.

There are fewer paintings on the left wall of the Gallery, but they include some of the finest in the cave. The painting nearest the entrance depicts a large slender red cow with a black head and a disproportionately long tail hanging down as far as the ledge (Plate 19). Its extremities are incomplete, but the rendering of thighs and chest is admirable. It is heading in the same direction as the leaping cow – towards the far end of the Gallery. The whole figure is about 9 ft long.

Beyond the cow with the black head and separated from it by the group of bistre and black horses and the red and black bovids of the vault, an enormous black bull is shown advancing with lowered head (Plate 18). Muzzle, neck, forelegs, and chest with a double fold of fat give an extraordinary impression of strength. The rendering of the hindquarters is less successful; the artist seems to have been hampered in his work by his effort to superimpose the body of the bull on existing paintings of bovids (Fig. 13). Four pairs of horns of a light bistre protrude beyond the line of the bull's back and several legs and a reddish rump are shown below and behind the animal. The horns belong to a series of four heads which formed a frieze: the bodies were probably never drawn. On monochrome photographs these heads are barely visible, but with strong lighting they are fairly easy to decipher on the spot. A careful study of the black filling-in of the bull's body reveals the shape of the two red bovids which it covers. The bull is about 10 ft long. In front of it there is a black three-branched sign beneath which the very faded silhouette of a bistre horse can be distinguished.

Beyond the bull two clumsily rendered equids face each other. They are thought to be wild asses. One is probably in foal, for it has an enormous swollen belly (Fig. 28). Both are painted in bistre, and the outlines and the manes are underlined in a darker bistre. They are among the rare figures in the

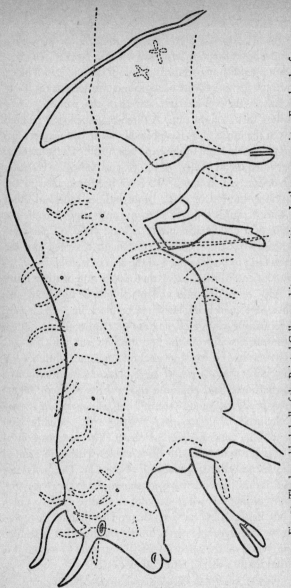

Fig. 13. The large black bull of the Painted Gallery and its superpositions. In the upper register: Four heads of bovids in bistre outline. In the lower register: Two slender cows painted in black and red. Length of bull from the nostrils to the root of the tail 10 ft. See Plate 18.

cave painted below the level of the cornice. Near these wild asses, and above them, a large horse some 10 ft in length is painted in a reddish nigger-brown colour outlined with black on an attractive snow-white background of calcite flakes (Plate 13). Some of these flakes are later than the painting, over which they form a light film. A three-branched sign painted in front of the horse's legs has probably some connexion with the sign painted in front of the large black bull. The horse may be superposed on an earlier red figure, and the sign overlaps a curious design which appears to have been stencilled in the same style as the red or black hand outlines found in other caves. This design is thought by some authorities * to be the silhouette of a child's arm placed on the wall and encircled with colour; but the spot is very difficult to reach and the shape too long to be the stencil of the arm of a child.

At the far end of the Gallery there is a group of three bistre horses with blurred manes and black hoofs, the head and shoulders of a small black horse, and a black line which may be the remaining vestige of the head of a horse. These figures cover the entire wall from the floor to the vault, which at this point is very low. Two thin chestnut-red lines with several branches start from a series of large black dots at the foot of one of the horses and continue above three of them. These lines may represent a long creeper; but, as vegetation is very rarely depicted in Palaeolithic art, they may equally well represent some entirely different object. The composition of two of the bistre horses with black manes which are painted one above the other is interesting (Plate 14). The belly and hindlegs of the upper horse are not shown; its forelegs are bent to avoid cutting across the neck of the horse below, and a white line has been left between them. This manner of representing two animals, one partly hidden by the other (a similar method is used on the opposite wall), is strange to us, but it is as valid as many other artistic conventions.

* Cf. H. Breuil, *Four Hundred Centuries of Cave Art*, p. 111.

The most interesting figure in this group is a bistre horse with black mane which is portrayed in the act of falling backwards, croup down, all four legs in the air (Plate 15). It is painted on a rock which juts out above the entrance to a narrow tunnel. This part of the Gallery is the most uneven and irregular area of the cave, and the rock-face forms an admirable natural setting: the impression of a horse falling into space is vividly conveyed.

The Gallery ends in a narrow twisting tunnel which begins at the level of the falling horse and is still partially blocked. At the time of the discovery there was only a very narrow space between the clay blocking and the roof. Some of the blocking was subsequently cleared ★ and, half crawling, half-crouching, it is now possible to penetrate the tunnel to a distance of about 18 yards. Beyond this point work has been held up and a mass of solid clay bars the way; there is just enough room between the roof and the blocking to insert an arm and shoulder and grope about with one's hand in the dark beyond; no one yet knows what lies there.

The roof of the tunnel is of sand-textured limestone which crumbles slightly between the fingers. For the first few yards the walls show a calcite exudation similar to that of the Great Hall and the Gallery; at one point this exudation covers even the roof, but it decreases progressively and soon comes to an end.

The light-coloured walls are not decorated; so it may have been blocked since Palaeolithic times. At the far end the sole signs of man's presence are large, irregular black spots which were probably made by the lamps of the excavators – acetylene lamps make such marks on cave walls after they have been hanging for some time. Some pinkish marks incrusted in the calcite appear to be old; they are possibly of natural origin.

★ The clearance was begun by Ravidat and Marsal and continued recently by Abbé Glory, but he was held up because of the difficulty of disposing of the débris. At the farthermost end he dug a small trench which yielded no trace of human presence.

Where the tunnel meets the Gallery some traces of red ochre are visible on the left-hand wall, but it is impossible to distinguish any outline. On the right-hand wall three animals are painted in Indian file as though they were coming out of the tunnel. The last animal in the file is in a bad state of preservation; tail, legs, and neck are barely distinguishable, but it has been identified as a horse, although the elongated hoofs look more like those of a bovid. It is painted in broad red bands which are somewhat blurred on each side. At this point the rock is covered with rounded bosses of white calcite. The majority of these bosses are of earlier date than the painting, but some of them cover it. The animal's eye is formed by a small circular hole about 2 in. deep which must be of natural formation, for the wall there is likewise covered with a thick layer of calcite which would not have had time to form if the hole had been made by man at the same time as the paintings. Perhaps this hole inspired the artist to place the animal's head at this point. Above the tail a sign in the form of an almost right-angled cross is painted in red ochre.

About 18 in. beyond this animal, a larger horse in a better state of preservation is painted just at the base of the rock wall and appears to be issuing from the depths of the earth to climb the side of the tunnel. A stroke which has scored the calcite outlines the back, and the eye and the muzzle are emphasized by the use of a darker ochre. The two small ears are shown as if seen full face. Below the figure the rock wall forms a narrow shelf on which there is an accumulation of dark pigments.

The horse is preceded by a bison which also appears to be climbing out of the entrance of the narrow tunnel (Plate 16). Like the horse, it is portrayed somewhat schematically by an outline of red bands which indicates an uplifted tail, sexual organ, and extremely rounded back. A black mark extends along the middle of the back. The head is not rendered with much detail and the horns are difficult to decipher, as they appear to be shown frontally like those of the bison in the cave of Marcenac (Plate 17). This red bison is painted immediately at the exit of the tunnel and faces the horse falling backwards.

THE LATERAL PASSAGE

To the right of the Hall of the Bulls, below the feet of the last of the large black bulls, a low rounded vault leads into a lateral passage which connects it with another part of the cave. Today the floor-level has been lowered and it is possible to stand upright in the Passage; but at the time of the discovery it was almost entirely blocked up with clay and was passable only by crawling on bent knees or on all fours. The saucer-like formations in the Great Hall of the Bulls extended into this passage for a few yards and indicated one of the courses of the stream from the entrance of the cave to the far end.

The walls of the vault are light in colour, even of surface, and of a sand-like texture similar to the walls of the narrow tunnel at the end of the Painted Gallery. They are much eroded and shed a fine powder at the slightest touch. An exudation of white calcite is found only at the base of the walls a few inches from the ground and immediately above the ledge, which at this point runs almost level with the floor. A few vestiges of paint have been preserved on these exudations, whereas the rock no longer shows any traces of coloured pigment. The importance of the part played by the calcite deposits in the extraordinary preservation of the Lascaux paintings can be realized here more clearly than in any other part of the cave. From one end of the Passage to the other the ledges show vivid red and black stains probably made by pigments which crumbled from earlier paintings, for it is likely that this Passage was once as richly decorated as the other chambers. Today only a few rare traces of paint are left owing to the friability of the walls and the current of air which blows over them. It is also possible that the coming and going of human beings in this Passage may have hastened the destruction of the paintings, for it is so narrow that they could not have avoided rubbing the walls with their bodies.

Traces of paint adhering to the calcite are found on each side of the entrance to the Lateral Passage. On the right there are the vestiges of at least two bovids – one red, the other of a darker colour. The legs and the belly painted on the calcite deposit are still visible, but no other traces remain. It is impossible, therefore, to say much more about the style of these animal paintings than that the very elongated cloven hoofs are represented frontally and show their two divisions. Hoofs are almost invariably depicted in this style in the Lascaux paintings. The legs and belly of a large black horse (it must have been about 7 ft in length), which are in a similar state of preservation to the figures on the right, are visible on the left-hand wall.

The first engravings of the cave are incised in the sand-textured limestone at a point some distance beyond these figures. Some of them are complete in themselves and others are combined with painting, although the traces of paint are so faint that they would be meaningless without the engraved line encircling them. As the rock is so friable, it is likely that the coloured pigments came away with the fine particles which crumbled from the rock-face. The engravings, on the contrary, particularly the deepest incisions, have been preserved where deterioration of the surface has not reached the depth of the incised line. It is possible that all these engravings may once have been painted.

A complete inventory of the engravings at Lascaux has never been published. Such an inventory is difficult to compile and involves an immense amount of patient work and a great deal of time.* The copying of all the engraved panels of the

* This task has been undertaken by Abbé Glory under the auspices of the Ministère des Beaux-Arts. It is not yet completed, but it has been possible to draw up an interim inventory of more than 600 figures (both paintings and engravings) from information kindly supplied by the Abbé himself.

cave line by line would be unsatisfactory, as it would result in a mere network of lines, most of them meaningless. However firm the intention to remain as objective as possible, it is difficult to avoid singling out and interpreting the most characteristic silhouettes. Some of the engraved panels may well seem a confused jumble of incised lines with no apparent characteristic features, but when a light is played upon the panels or arranged to fall obliquely on them in such a way as to accentuate the shadows, it is moderately easy to distinguish a few essential outlines (cf. Plates 23 and 24). Most of the outlines are broken and incomplete, however, and without great experience of Palaeolithic art their interpretation is impossible. Certain outlines are completely incomprehensible and cannot be linked to any known animal silhouettes. The deciphering of these engravings is made even more difficult in certain parts of the cave, particularly in the Gallery beyond the Lateral Passage, by the fact that the animal figures are often covered with a network of incomprehensible strokes. In such cases an examination of first-class photographs under a magnifying glass will often reveal details which were overlooked when the engravings were examined on the walls with the naked eye.

In the Lateral Passage certain engravings are superposed one on the other, but these are easier to distinguish than those on some of the panels in the Gallery beyond it. When there is difficulty in deciphering a figure, it is due more to the worn surface of the rock than to the medley of animal figures which have been neither scored nor scratched. In fact, in certain places the rock is so worn that the engraved lines have almost disappeared and the shadows thrown by an oblique light are very faint. The most noteworthy figures in the Lateral Passage are a fine head of a bovid painted in red and engraved; numerous horses still bearing traces of red or black paint whose outstandingly black hoofs in particular have successfully withstood the ravages of time; some bovids and some small ibex heads. There are very few signs in the Passage.

THE CHAMBER OF ENGRAVINGS

The Lateral Passage leads close to the beginning of a vast elbowed Gallery. On some parts of its walls there is a jumble of engraved and painted and engraved figures, and on others there are friezes which show relatively few superpositions. Some of the figures, like those in the first part of the cave, are painted only.

Where the Lateral Passage joins the Main Gallery a small semi-circular chamber opens out to the right: this is the Chamber of Engravings. The walls appear to be different in texture from the walls of the Lateral Passage: they are harder and firmer, and no exudation of calcite is apparent. Lines radiate in all directions over earlier black paintings now almost completely obliterated. Their interpretation is difficult, and the inventory of figures in this part of the cave has not yet been completed.

The most important and the clearest figures consist of groups of the same species which form friezes – files of ibexes or antelopes, groups of horses, bovids, or deer in various attitudes. The isolated figures seem to bear no relation to the animals surrounding them or to those on which they are superposed.

The earliest figures in this intricate medley are the largest. Three groups at least can be distinguished. High on the walls which form a cupola there are remains of a magnificent frieze of painted and engraved deer. These figures are difficult to distinguish, but when they have been deciphered the skill of the composition and the grace of the contours compel admiration. Especially noteworthy are a deer with chestnut-red horns and black hoofs which has been wounded in the body (Fig. 14), two deer painted in chestnut and black which enframe it, and a magnificent beast with large upraised antlers rendered in a style somewhat different from that of the other deer in the cave (see Fig. 22a).

Traces of a few large black bovids are discernible below the

Fig. 14. Wounded deer painted and engraved on a wall in the Chamber of Engravings. The body has almost vanished, but the hoofs and the antlers are clearly visible. In front of it there is a painted and engraved horse. The tail is attached to the body in precisely the same way as the tails of the bistre and black horse on Plate 10, and the horse in front of the imaginary animal on Plate 2 etc.

frieze of deer from which they are separated by a natural formation of the rock, horses are painted and engraved on the vaulted roof, and, at the farthermost end of the Chamber, on a level with the frieze of large deer, a series of smaller deer is engraved (Plate 23).

Most of the animals bear superposed engravings of smaller more recent figures. Some very fine deer are superimposed on earlier paintings of black bovids which are partially scored and scratched and almost illegible. The engraved outlines of the deer (Plate 22) stand out clearly against the black of the earlier bovids. On the same panel clusters of divergent lines form designs of a type frequently found in Palaeolithic art and known as 'huts'.

In 1949 a new explanation of these designs was put forward; * it was suggested that they might represent Palaeolithic sorcerers clothed in a ceremonial costume made of long grasses similar to that worn by Negro sorcerers in French Guinea. This disguise is made of plaited fibres splaying from a sort of disc at the top, also made of plaited fibres, which forms a head-dress. This explanation is ingenious, for, if a photograph of a sorcerer dressed in this costume is compared with one of the Lascaux designs, the resemblance is indeed strikingly apparent. At the top of one of these designs there seems also to be a suggestion of a human face; but a closer examination shows that it is a mere accidental formation due to traces of underlying black paintings, and not a deliberate portrayal of human features. It is so easy to see faces, especially human faces, in rock formations, branches, clouds, etc., and therefore it seems prudent to refrain from jumping to conclusions. It has been suggested that the small horse's head emerging from a cluster of parallel lines which is painted in the same part of the cave represents a sorcerer with a horse's head; but this interpretation seems an unlikely one. Such hypotheses would be worth investigation only if other human or animal faces were discovered in the 'huts' already known at Altamira and elsewhere.

THE MAIN GALLERY

At its junction with the Chamber of Engravings, the Lateral Passage curves to the left into a vast gallery with a lofty ceiling and a floor sloping steeply downwards towards the far end (Plate 21). When the cave was discovered, this floor was broken by a funnel-shaped aperture similar to that in the Great Hall of the Bulls, but this is now filled in. At some unknown time the clay blocking was gradually sucked down to the

---

* H. Breuil, *Four Hundred Centuries of Cave Art*, pp. 146–7.

lower galleries through this 'suction pit', and possibly through others which have not been revealed, and the floor thus lowered to a level considerably below that of the Great Hall, the Lateral Passage, and the Chamber of Engravings.

The Main Gallery is fairly regular in shape, and widens out above the cornice like a funnel. It is about 27 yards long and its width varies from 1 yard to $3\frac{1}{4}$ yards. At its loftiest point, near the farthermost end, the vault must be about 22 ft high – perhaps even higher. Owing to the slope of the ground, the cornice is almost at floor level at the point where the Passage joins the Gallery, but it rises abruptly to a height well above arm's length. Almost all the figures are placed above this cornice, and therefore the Palaeolithic artists must certainly have used some kind of scaffolding of branches in order to carry out their work, although, as suggested by Breuil, when they drew their figures the floor level may have been higher than it is today. The cornices are blackish and irregular, like those in the first chambers. Above them, the walls and the vault are smooth and light in colour and bear no traces of exudation.

The engravings of the left-hand wall of the Lateral Passage continue on the left-hand wall of the Gallery without a break. The first figures on a panel with lopped-off corners are two

Fig. 15. Horse's head engraved at the entrance to the Main Gallery.

Fig. 16. Group of five horses and one bison painted and engraved at the entrance to the Main Gallery. The engraving of the bison seems to show different versions of the head. Length of the first horse on the left 3 ft 8 in.; length of the bison 4 ft 5 in. See Plate 29.

fine horses engraved one above the other. One head in particular is outstanding (Fig. 15). At some distance from these horses a frieze of attractive painted and engraved ibex heads can be deciphered in spite of the worn state of the wall (Plates 26, 27, and Fig. 2). It consists of four black heads with long chestnut-red horns at the left-hand side followed by three red heads at the right-hand side. The paint on the engraved horns of the red heads is no longer visible. The frieze is now very faded, but its decorative effect must once have been astonishing.

Below and to one side of the frieze of ibexes, a group consisting of horses and bison is painted and engraved in a niche of the wall (Plates 20, 28a, and Fig. 16). This group is arranged on two levels: three horses and a bison on the upper level, and two horses on the lower level. The balance of the composition on the upper level is striking – the three horses are arranged on one side advancing towards a latticed sign and on the other the bison is shown advancing towards a similar latticed sign. The first horse, about 3 ft 7 in. long, is moving with outstretched neck towards the Passage. It is painted in black with light-coloured spaces in the region of the belly, and these light-coloured spaces are separated from the dark parts by small hatchings. The mane is also indicated by hatchings. A dart is painted on its croup and two strokes are shown across its swollen belly.

This figure, which may represent a pregnant mare, is followed by a galloping horse about 3 ft 8 in. long, painted chestnut-red and black with an exaggeratedly puffed-out mane. Like those of many horses in the cave, its mane, hoofs, and fetlock joints are painted an intense black and appear to be in a better state of preservation and later in date than the rest of the painting; but the fresher appearance may be due to the fact that black is less prone to deterioration than other pigments. A black line may indicate the phallus. The figure is pierced by seven parallel darts pointing upwards, and an eighth and shorter dart is shown embedded in the region of its chest. The third horse is smaller in size, with a reddish-brown body and black head and mane. The hindquarters are engraved over the hindquarters of a male bison, likewise painted and engraved, facing in the opposite direction. The two animals are shown with their croups overlapping in a symmetrical and obviously carefully planned pattern. The bison, which is about 4 ft 5 in. in length, is painted brown with black legs. Its body is pierced by seven deeply engraved darts and overlaid with a few incised lines difficult to decipher. Below the bison and the three horses described, two horses of the same style, but smaller in size, are painted and engraved; one is painted in black, the other in black and brown.

The entire frieze of five horses and one bison is about 15 ft long. It is somewhat hidden in a recess, and its dimensions are modest in comparison with the frieze following it, which extends along the middle of the wall to a total length of about 33 ft (Plate 30). The central subject of this vast frieze is an enormous black cow (about 5 ft long), whose massive body is in striking contrast with its slender legs and head, flanked by several horses. It was painted in the first place and then engraved, and the engraved line outlining it stands out sharply in white. Both its hindlegs are placed on a latticed sign similar to those in other parts of the cave, but depicted with more care: all the details are engraved and painted in several colours. A third sign is painted slightly behind it on a level with the cow's tail and touching a small brown horse.

The long frieze of horses was executed at an earlier date than the black cow, for several of the horses are covered by the cow (Plates 28b, 29, 31, and 32). It is difficult to say whether the cow was superposed on these figures for reasons of convenience or whether the superposition was a deliberate part of the whole composition. Whatever the reason, all the figures are painted and engraved in a style which appears to be identical, and there is no doubt that they belong to the same artistic period.

All the horses of the frieze except the first one are facing in the opposite direction to the cow and are depicted galloping or walking – some of them in double file. They are all painted in tones of chestnut-bistre and black and are also engraved. Their average length is about 3 ft and the frieze covers a large part of the Gallery. A rapid examination reveals five animals in front of the cow, four others behind it, and one below its tail. Other figures are more difficult to decipher, either because they are superposed one over the other, or because they are almost concealed by the cow. One small animal is engraved in the belly of another and might be interpreted as a very elementary representation of a foetus (Plate 31). Several heads are visible; they may be different versions of the head of one animal, but it is more likely that they are the heads of several animals running alongside each other. A magnificent rearing horse is painted inside the cow (Fig. 17). Originally there were probably two figures, for a second mane more or less parallel to the first is discernible slightly behind it. In addition, two very fine horses' heads (Plate 31) protrude from the rump of the cow, and their brownish-red bodies are visible within its body. It is unlikely that one of the figures is a correction of the other: the painting undoubtedly portrays two horses galloping side by side. The entire frieze consists of at least seventeen horses.

Towards the back of the Gallery, comparatively close to the last horse, two magnificent brown male bison are shown back to back (Plate 41). They are painted below the level of the cornice, but the limestone rock at that spot is smooth and light in colour. These are the last figures on the left-hand wall.

The right-hand wall is more difficult of access, because the ledge there is steep and lofty. It is decorated with one frieze only. A single file of heads of deer in profile is painted in black line several yards above floor level (Plate 33). It is probable that the artist intended to depict a herd swimming across a river, and the edge of the ledge represents the water-line. The first deer in the file is very skilfully portrayed in the act of throwing back its head, as if about to climb out of the water on to land (Plate 42). This representation is unique in cave art. A small bistre horse with ruffled mane underlies these deers' heads.

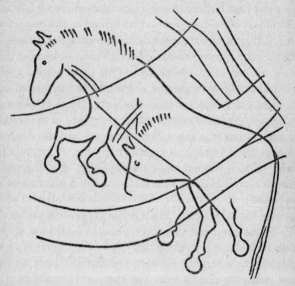

Fig. 17. Rearing horse engraved within the large black cow in the Main Gallery (Plate 32). It is intersected by several lines among which the two parallel lines of the cow's belly and at least one head and a leg of other horses can be distinguished. Some parallel lines behind this figure are possibly incomplete outlines or traces of other horses depicted in a similar attitude.

THE CHAMBER OF FELINES

The frieze of deer is painted opposite the cow and the chequered signs. A little farther on the rock walls narrow and the slope of the floor becomes steeper. Immediately beyond the two powerful silhouettes of the bison painted back to back there is a narrow passage whose walls are covered with decomposed white concretions which are soft to the touch and crumble between the fingers. These thick trails of 'moon-milk' come from the extremely lofty roof. Neither engravings nor paintings are possible on this fragile surface. The ground is damp; when it rains the drops can be heard falling one by one in the silence of the cave.

The two 'moon-milk' coated walls are so close that they practically meet and form a low vault that has to be entered on all fours. The cave seems to end at this point, but in fact a narrow corridor continues beyond it and the floor-level rises to a sort of steeply ascending tunnel hollowed in the rock. After a rise of a few yards the tunnel continues on a more horizontal level, then broadens into a succession of small irregular alcoves whose sides are decorated with several painted and engraved figures.

Although this part of the cave is remote and difficult of access, it received no less attention from the artists than chambers which are more accessible or more easily viewed. Indeed, the paintings and engravings have been executed with equal skill and the subjects are sometimes somewhat different from the others in the cave – an indication that for Palaeolithic Man this tunnel had a special significance. The outstanding figures in the first small alcove are a series of engraved latticed signs similar to those beneath the feet of the large black cow, an engraved horse and a group of felines, one of them pierced by seven darts, which is extremely difficult to interpret (Plate 34 and Fig. 18). There are also two very fine engraved and painted horses in bistre and black running side by side and a magnificent bovid with upraised tail in an attitude of rage. Beyond these figures there are vestiges of a painting which may have been gradually rubbed off by constant friction against the walls of the extremely narrow passage. Now, the intensely black hoofs and joints are almost the only traces left of a very faded bistre horse. They stand out vividly against the light wall, and it is amusing to conjecture how these black

Fig. 18. Three felines engraved in the Chamber of Felines. See Plate 34.

blobs might have been interpreted had they been discovered some thousands of years later after all other traces of paint had disappeared. Below them there are paintings of other bistre and black horses, two of which may be coupled. Between the horse on the upper level and those below it a long, slightly undulating band composed of short parallel strokes in brownish-red almost encircles the alcove. Its significance is uncertain: it may represent some kind of lasso with which to catch horses.

On the inside of the small dome which forms the roof of this alcove four strokes which could be interpreted as darts are engraved. Below the level of the engravings the walls are blackened, but not by contact with human bodies, for the black marks are more abundant on horizontal surfaces where contact could only be accidental. These black traces and those in other chambers are undoubtedly made by particles of pigment which fell from early paintings and gradually settled on the walls in the still air.

Farther on, the floor of the tunnel ends abruptly in a chasm several feet deep and the head of a painted bison at a low point on the vertical wall has been reported. The gap over the chasm can be crossed without difficulty because the rock there has gradually been worn to the shape of a gigantic sponge whose cavities provide an easy hold. Beyond it the tunnel continues. There is nothing to be seen on its walls apart from a few dark red dots and an engraved figure with a slight resemblance to the Roman figure XIII. Soon it becomes narrower, and finally contracts into an impassable fissure blocked with clay. No one has ever tried to clear this fissure, and no one knows where it leads to; it was probably impenetrable even in Palaeolithic times.

On the right of the tunnel there is a narrow cleft which can be entered, but here, too, the floor ends suddenly in a steep drop. The walls are very damp. Two or three yeards below, a floor of sodden sand and gravel indicates the bed of an intermittent stream which probably finds its way into the lower levels of the cave. It is easy to clamber down to this bed, but upstream and downstream the walls close in almost immediately, and it is impossible to continue any farther. There are no traces of any Palaeolithic art on the walls, but they are so damp that no paintings could possibly have been preserved on them for any length of time.

THE SHAFT OF THE DEAD MAN

The deep, irregular holes beyond the Chamber of Felines have not laid bare any secret in spite of the importance which Palaeolithic Man clearly attached to this part of the cave. The conditions are somewhat similar to those prevailing at the other end of the Main Gallery, where the most amazing scene in the entire cave is painted. To reach it one must retrace one's steps from the Chamber of Felines, return along the passage with 'moon-milk'-coated walls, and pass between the black cow and the chain of horses on one side and the frieze of swimming deer on the other. Leaving the entrance to the Lateral Passage which leads into the Hall of the Bulls on the right, one continues towards the elbowed part of the Main Gallery called the Chamber of Engravings, which appears to end in a cul-de-sac. At first sight this Chamber seems to be one of the least impressive parts of the cave, for the walls are marked and scored in all directions. But this concentration of confused lines and figures which are very difficult to decipher may indicate, on the contrary, that the place was particularly sacred or important. The walls are covered up to the vault with a medley of engraved figures superposed on earlier red or black paintings; among them are some unusual representations of large 'huts', and networks of engraved lines. The decorated walls have a patina; worn and smoothed by time and friction, they bear witness to the constant use and frequentation of this part of the cave.

At the far end of the Chamber of Engravings, a stone, highly polished, worn, and much blackened by the constant passage of countless human bodies, forms a kind of lip over a yawning pit. The domed vault above it is engraved with various animal figures, latticed signs painted in several colours, long bands of short parallel strokes, and clusters of diverging lines similar to those in the Chamber, but of smaller size (Plate 23). The quintessence of all the signs in the cave would seem to be concentrated on the restricted surface of this dome, in spite of the fact that it is so high above the Shaft leading down to the well and the scene of the Dead Man and must have been very difficult to reach.

At the bottom of this shaft, which is about 16 ft deep, and must once have had to be negotiated by means of a rope, there is a small irregular chamber formed by a fault in the rock which is partially filled with clay. At each end the fault extends into long fissures, one of which has been cleared and is now accessible. The walls of the chamber are almost entirely covered with a thin coating of hardened clay, and in certain places where there is a slight exudation of calcite they sparkle. Parts of this calcite formation are of later date than the paintings.

There is very little decoration on the walls. On the right-hand there is a painting of a small black horse's head with a blurred mane, but it attracts little notice because all attention is focused on the painted panel about 6 ft 6 in. in length immediately at the base of the Shaft (Plate 35). The central figure is a bird-headed man drawn in black outline and very stiff in contrast with the supple lines of the other figures in the cave. The body is a mere rectangle with a black stroke indicating the phallus. Each arm is represented by a single stroke ending in a four-fingered hand, and the legs and feet, which are merely bent extensions of the legs, are not rendered in any detail. At the man's side lies a hooked stick; in front of him the schematized figure of a bird, likewise outlined in black, with a head precisely similar to his own, is perched on a pole which ends in a few short black vertical strokes.

The man appears to be falling backwards. In front of him a bison rendered in a somewhat unusual style awkwardly turns its head, probably the better to threaten him with its horns. It is painted in black outline and its mane is depicted by a series of black parallel strokes. The interior of the body is brown, but it has not been painted – the artist has cunningly placed his bison where the clay is of a darker colour than the rest of the wall, and here and there this discoloration extends beyond the silhouette of the bison. The animal is shown thrashing the air with its tail, which is stiffly and clumsily rendered. It is badly wounded, and its entrails are hanging from its body in large black loops. A long spear, probably the Bird-Headed Man's, is shown lying across its body over the wound.

To the left of the Man a rhinoceros with two horns – the only rhinoceros in the cave – is shown moving away from the scene (Plate 35). This figure is lightly modelled in black, and in style is therefore closer to the paintings in the Great Hall of the Bulls and the Painted Gallery than to the Bird-Headed Man or the wounded bison. If in fact it is part of the scene, it does not seem to have been painted by the same hand; nor is the technique similar to that of the other figures.

The painting is clearly incomplete, for the outlines of the belly, chest, and foreleg have been merely sketched in black line and never filled in. Under the upraised tail there are six black dots of doubtful significance. and slightly below them some black marks which may be traces of the imprint of a hand. Could it be the hand of the artist? Thousands and thousands of years ago, did he thoughtlessly place it, blackened with pigment, on the walls he had just been painting?

CHAPTER 2

THE DATE OF LASCAUX

THE date of Lascaux within the framework of Franco-Cantabrian wall art can be estimated in two ways: first, by a study of the archaeological remains which have been found in the cave; second, by a study of the styles and superpositions of the paintings and engravings in relation to the known stages of cave art. The results arrived at can only be approximate, however, because of the uncertain nature of the chronological framework of the evolution of Palaeolithic art (see pp. 29–43).

Archaeological Evidence

In the early days of the cave's discovery, Monsieur Laval, the retired schoolmaster of Montignac, made a few finds in the cave, but they were of somewhat limited interest. On the left-hand ledge of the Main Gallery, for example, he found three natural saucer-shaped stones which had lain forgotten for many thousands of years and could only have been placed there by Man. Some blackish marks which resembled the deposit of a grease lamp were found on two of them, and in the third were two small flat stones, one of them marked with black, which have been interpreted as a mortar and a colour palette. Dozens of similar stones were subsequently found in the Shaft of the Dead Man; so it is probable that all of them were merely specimens of the innumerable lamps used to light the cave during the painting of the walls or in the course of the ceremonies which took place there.

In addition, some flint tools were found lying just under the surface of the clay,★ below the bison and the horses pierced by darts which are engraved at the point where the Lateral Passage leads into the Main Gallery (Fig. 16). They were mainly blades and small blades, most of them broken and none of them of any particular type. It is difficult to assign them to any specific period: they might be Early Magdalenian.

In 1940, when Abbé Breuil wished to photograph certain figures in the Great Hall of the Bulls, he had to empty out the water filling the rimmed saucer-like formations by piercing their bases at various points in order to be able to place the camera in a suitable position. Under the calcite crust, in a sodden layer of clay mixed with the gravel carried in by the water which drained in from the plateau, a few flakes of worked flint, some remains of reindeer bone, and some fragments of conifer charcoal were revealed. Outside the course of the stream he found small heaps of charcoal only partially covered by the soil.† All that can be said about these finds is that they are Late Palaeolithic: they add nothing to the existing knowledge of the cave's age and merely prove that the soil of the floor of the Great Hall has changed very little since Palaeolithic Man last used the cave.

A few years after the discovery, when circumstances permitted, excavations ‡ were undertaken in the Shaft of the Dead Man by Abbé Breuil and Monsieur S. Blanc, Director of Prehistoric Antiquities of the Region, the centre of which is Les Eyzies, for it was hoped – not without reason – that some burial which would reveal the meaning of the scene painted on the wall would be found.

★ In 1948 Monsieur Laval sent a collection of small-sized flints from this site to the Musée de l'Homme for examination. It included a dozen blades and fragments of blades, which were not very typical; twenty-three small blades and fragments of small blades, two of them with blunted edges and one retouched at one edge only; one small round scraper and two large flakes. All these finds were probably collected by him alone.

† H. Breuil, 'Lascaux', S.P.F., Nos. 6, 7, 8 (June, July, August) 1950.

‡ See Gallia, 1948, pp. 395–8.

The 'Shaft' is, in fact, a fault in the limestone which is partially filled by a mass of clay and a variety of débris several feet thick. This fault extends to the left in a narrow fissure which could be penetrated even before its clearance had been undertaken. The floor of this narrow fissure rises steeply, and since its clearance it has been possible to enter a chamber at the top of the slope which was never frequented by Palaeolithic Man. The roof of this chamber must be close to the surface of the plateau, for a few tree-roots have forced their way through it. Further excavation was suspended because of the danger of a fall of rock, but in any case it seems unlikely that it would have led to any discovery of interest.

To the left, an extension of the floor of the small chamber has been cleared of a mass of sand and clay to a height of about 7 ft. It consisted of only one archaeological level, which contained a large number of somewhat irregular pieces of limestone clearly selected by Palaeolithic Man because of their flat or slightly concave shape and then carried by him to the interior of the cave. These stones were produced by the exfoliation of the limestone of the plateau and they are abundant in the vicinity. Most of the specimens found bore black marks in the centre of the hollow and in some instances traces of conifer charcoal. They are undoubtedly primitive handlamps similar to those found in the Main Gallery.

These handlamps present a curious problem: not in themselves, as it is clear that the artists who executed the frescoes must have used some kind of illumination and a certain number of Palaeolithic lamps is already known, but because of the place where they were found. Why was there such an accumulation of them in such a remote corner of the cave? They cannot have been lamps thrown away after each use, because in that case they would have been found scattered all over the cave. The hypothesis that the cave was cleaned up after the paintings had been completed is equally unsatisfactory; for Palaeolithic Man, like the majority of present-day primitives, allowed kitchen waste and various débris to accumulate in his occupation sites, and such a regard for cleanliness would be exceptional. In addition, the Bird-Headed Man, the wounded enraged bison, and the rhinoceros must have been especially sacred and awe-inspiring figures of particular significance; therefore it is highly improbable that the Shaft where they are painted would have been used as a waste-pit for the disposal of useless objects. Large quantities of conifer charcoal were found in association with the lamps, some rather uncharacteristic flint débris, and some spears in deer horn. These spears provide an interesting guide for the study of the significance of the cave; as it was neither a workshop nor a dwelling-place, it is clear that they were used in some ritual connected with the paintings.

All these finds came from one level only. From the typological point of view, only the spears can be dated, but with no certainty, because of the absence of any other objects. Some authorities attribute them to Late Perigordian, others to very Early Magdalenian, prior to Magdalenian III. According to both these hypotheses, the spears, and probably the scene in the Shaft and the whole of the paintings and engravings in the cave, belong to that period in Palaeolithic art which corresponds to the end of the Perigordian and the beginning of the Magdalenian.

Further excavation has been undertaken more recently by Abbé Glory both at the far end of the tunnel which terminates the Painted Gallery and in the Chamber of Felines. Nothing was found in the tunnel, but some remains came to light in the Chamber of Felines. When clearing the blocking in one of the small alcoves in the Chamber of Felines, Abbé Glory found a few somewhat untypical flints, a reindeer metatarsus and shin-bone and a fragment of carbonized rope. The rope was embedded in the clay and its imprint was very clear. The fact that this is the first remains of plaiting dating from the Reindeer Age ever found gives the find an especial interest, but it precludes any typological comparisons.* At the bottom of the Shaft, beyond the Chamber of Felines, a flint was found, and an excavation made at the end of the tunnel beyond the shaft revealed a hearth containing a few horse bones.

These scanty data are fortunately complemented by the dating of the charcoal found in association with the lamps and the spears in the Shaft of the Dead Man. This charcoal was sent to Professor Libby's laboratory in Chicago to be dated by the study of the radio-active isotopes of carbon (C14), for at that time no laboratory in Europe was equipped for these dating tests. An examination of the charcoal established an approximate age of 15,000 years (15,515 years to be exact) † with a possible margin of error of ±900 years. This was the first positive dating of Late Palaeolithic remains in Western Europe to be obtained by this or any other method. Despite the reservations which must be made with regard to a method the accuracy of which has still to be assessed for the dating of remains earlier than eight to ten millennia, such a chronological guide is of the greatest interest.

It is known that the last Magdalenians became extinct in Europe through emigration or through fusion with new elements at the very end of the last glaciation, i.e. about 10,000 years before the beginning of the Christian era, perhaps even a

* Abbé Glory. 'Débris de corde paléolithique à la grotte de Lascaux', S.P.F., 1956, p. 263-4.

† It would have been interesting to check and confirm the date arrived at by the testing of the charcoal from the Shaft by submitting the charcoal found in the Great Hall at the time of its discovery to a similar test. The latter must have been contemporaneous with the last Palaeolithic man to frequent the cave. It cannot be of earlier date than the last frequentation of this underground sanctuary, for, if frequentation had continued after the extinguishing of the hearths, the charcoal would have been crushed, scattered, and destroyed. Conversely, it is improbable that the hearths were kindled a long time after the last ceremonies had taken place in the cave, for the archaeological remains found belong only to one particular epoch; and if the entrance had remained accessible for a long time, the preservation of the paintings would undoubtedly have suffered. The charcoal collected by Abbé Glory in the Chamber of Felines has been sent to London for dating.

little later. It is generally supposed, however, that the evolution of the Magdalenian industry was spread over a greater number of millennia than is suggested by the date of the Lascaux charcoal. If that date (13,000 B.C.) is correct, and if indeed it corresponds to the late Perigordian or the early Magdalenian industries, then the evolution of this culture cannot have extended over more than about five millennia, i.e. from 14,000 or 13,000 B.C. to 9000 or 8000 B.C.

From their style and technique, the paintings and engravings at Lascaux are attributed by Breuil to the peak period of Perigordian art, which has generally been estimated at about 20,000 B.C. at least. The sudden advancing of the date of the Perigordian by about 7,000 years is difficult to explain. Several hypotheses can be put forward. It might be suggested, for example, that the charcoal and the industry associated with the scene in the Shaft have no connexion with the paintings and engravings of the cave as a whole, or even with the Bird-Headed Man, the bison, and the rhinoceros. This hypothesis is difficult to accept, for who but the artists who decorated the cave, or those who subsequently made use of the paintings and engravings, could have left behind them, in that remote fissure, so many lamps and such abundant traces of charcoal? Another hypothesis might postulate that the carbon dating is inaccurate, and thus completely nullify the others. A third hypothesis might suppose that the cave of Lascaux is accurately dated by the charcoal test, in which case either the date of the Perigordian culture would be much later than that accepted hitherto, and consequently the beginning of the Magdalenian era would be correspondingly advanced or else Lascaux should be dated to the beginning of the Magdalenian. As far as Palaeolithic art is concerned, the gap between the Aurignacio-Perigordian cycle and the Solutreo-Magdalenian cycle is not confirmed by new discoveries, which seem to indicate that the interval between works of art attributed to late Perigordian and those attributed to Magdalenian III may not have been very long. Since the fauna at Lascaux indicates a fairly temperate climate, the date of Lascaux would have to coincide with one of the temperate oscillations which characterized the end of the last glacial period. The dates of these have not yet been conclusively established.*

It is impossible to solve these problems and establish a conclusive dating for Lascaux without undertaking further excavations and submitting other organic remains of the same period for dating by C14. In the meantime it seems reasonable to accept as a working hypothesis the assumption that the cave of Lascaux as a whole dates from about 15,000 years ago without specifying the exact place in time of the paintings and engravings solely on the study of the archaeological evidence.

The Study of the Superpositions

According to the generally accepted theory, the study of the superpositions of paintings and engravings of different ages enables the sequence of the various artistic periods to be established. First of all, the principal types of technique and the order of the superpositions are determined, and then a comparison is made with the sequences established in other caves. This method has been abused, however, and certain figures have sometimes been attributed to various artistic periods, whereas in fact they merely represent different stages in the

* Cf. Breuil, 'Les datations par le C14 de Lascaux (Dordogne) et de Philip Caves (S.W. Africa)', *S.P.F.*, vol. li, fasc. 11-12, Dec. 1954, pp. 544-9. 'Même à supposer que la suite donne raison à M. Blanc (que Lascaux soit Magdalénien ancien) et en tenant compte de ce que les charbons sont vraisemblablement de la fin de l'occupation, cela ne laisserait, si l'on admet que le Magdalénien supérieur (IV à VI) ou tout le Magdalénien et Solutréen sont encore d'âge glaciaire, que 5.000 ans pour leur évolution, ce qui me paraît trop peu. Comme les essence d'arbres dont témoignent les charbons, comme la faune figurée de Lascaux excluent un tel maximum de froid, il n'y a pas lieu de retarder, mais de reculer l'âge de la fréquentation de la caverne.' This rules out the hypothesis of a temperate oscillation at about 13,000 B.C. (Cf. the following chapter on this subject, pp. 148-54.)

actual execution of a painting.* In addition, some representations have been described as superpositions instead of being interpreted as deliberately associated figures and carefully composed animal groups. In subsequent pages the reasons for the writer's belief in the great stylistic and chronological homogeneity of the Lascaux paintings will be set forth. The classic study of the superpositions remains indispensable, however, and will be further examined in an effort to regroup those paintings which seem to be contemporaneous rather than to seek to multiply the stages of development.

Apart from those in the Chamber of Engravings, the superpositions at Lascaux are not particularly numerous, and in spite of the close decoration of certain panels, there are many isolated paintings. In some superpositions the colouring matter is so well preserved that the underlying animal figure is still decipherable through the figure covering it. Nevertheless, the deciphering of superpositions is difficult, for in certain cases the two layers of colouring matter are irregularly superposed one on the other, and it is not easy to distinguish which is the earlier. Lighting conditions are a very important factor in the study of superpositions. An adjustable oblique light is best for the study of the engravings, and a strong direct light essential for the study of the paintings; the electric lighting of the cave has revealed numerous details which were overlooked in the early examinations of the paintings. Colour and infra-red photographs bring out certain details, but the 'Woods' lamp,†

---

* For example, certain outlines on one and the same panel have sometimes been described as linear drawings of a primitive phase underlying figures of a more complicated technique, whereas they might equally well be regarded as incomplete sketches made prior to the final painting proper.

† The region of the spectrum corresponding to the wavelengths of approximately 3,600 Ångstrom units can be isolated by means of special filters which absorb the visible radiation. This filtered radiation or 'Woods' lamp excites the fluorescence of certain substances and enables them to be actually seen. In archaeological layers the 'Woods' lamp enables the occupation levels rich in organic matter to be distinguished from sterile levels. This method of analysis is likewise used in the study of the paintings.

General view of the left-hand wall of the Great Hall of the Bulls. Facing each other are two large black bulls in black bands in more or less modelled technique; on the left a file of small black horses and a larger red horse with black head and legs (Plate 3). Between and above the two bulls the head and shoulders of a bistre and black horse; below it a group of five small deer (Plate 4). In the belly of the large bull on the right a red cow facing in the opposite direction (Fig. 10). The intrusion on the photograph (top right-hand corner) of the horns of two large black bulls is due to the domed shape of the Hall. See pp. 64 – 70.

1

The imaginary animal in the
Great Hall of the Bulls.
One part of it is covered by
a black headless horse, the
rock surface on which the
head was painted having
eroded and fallen to the
ground. Note the position
of the root of the horse's tail
and how the tail outlines
the front of the imaginary
animal's foreleg.
Length 5 ft 5 ins.
See pp. 65 – 6.

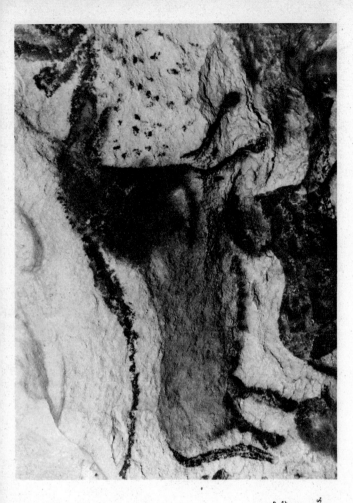

Red horse with black head, tail, and legs painted on the flank of one of the bulls of the Great Hall. Note the two heads. Length 9 ft 4 ins. See Plate 1 and page 66.

3

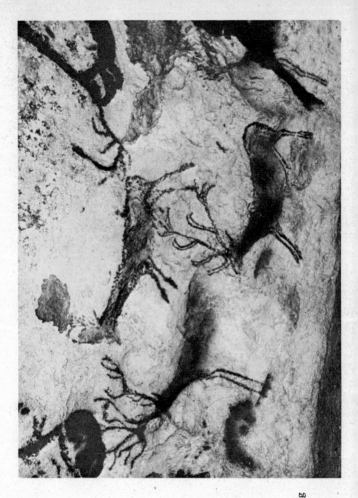

Group of small deer in
tones of bistre and black.
The horns of the topmost
deer are outlined by a flaking
of the rock. Length of each
deer about 2 ft 10 ins.
See Plate 1 and page 67.

4

Detail of one of the bulls
of the Great Hall.
See Plates 1 and 4 and
page 67.

5

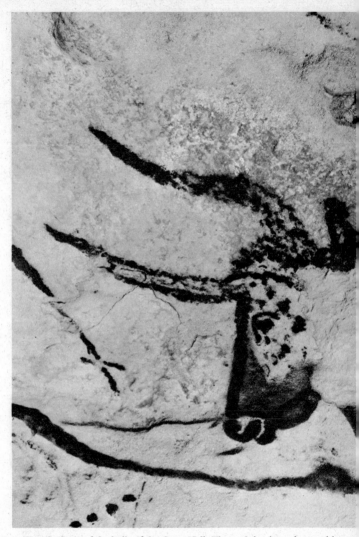

Detail of one of the bulls of the Great Hall. The neck has been damaged by the flaking of the rock. The dorsal line of another bull is visible below the nostrils. Several signs and punctuations. See page 68.

Vaulted roof of the Painted Gallery. Three red and black bovids and several bistre and black horses (only one is visible on the photograph) painted on the white ground of the vault. In the centre, a rough sketch in red line of a horse's head. Arrows and various signs. Almost all the flakings are of earlier date than the paintings. See pp. 72 - 3.

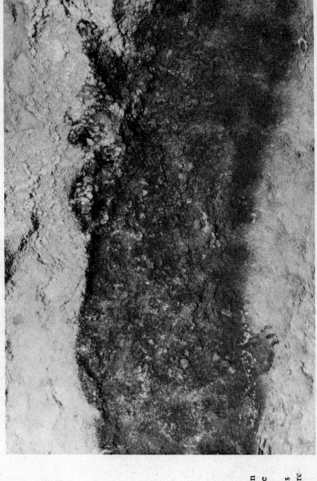

Small brown bear hidden in the belly of one of the bulls of the Great Hall. One hind paw and claws and the snout and ears are visible. See page 68.

Detail of one of the cows of Plate 7. In the lower right-hand corner a bistre and black horse. Numerous signs. A geometrical sign of the latticed type is discernible under the cow's tail. Length of cow 6 ft 8 ins. See pp. 72–3.

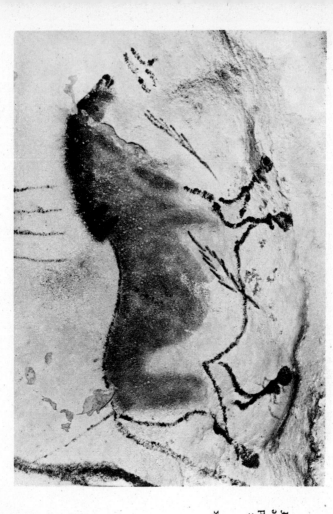

One of the bistre and black horses surrounded by painted arrows. Some flakings are of more recent date than those on the head and rump. Above the horse there is a geometric sign of the latticed type.
Length 4 ft 8 ins.
See pp. 72–3.

Deer with large antlers painted at the entrance to the Painted Gallery. The rough outline and the different dabs of colour from which the paint was spread can be seen. In the bottom left-hand corner a black rectangular sign; to the right a small three-legged horse (see Fig. 12). Height 4 ft 8 ins.
See pp. 71 – 2.

Panel on the right-hand
wall of the Painted Gallery.
In the centre a black cow
appears to be leaping over
a very large latticed sign.
Below it, to the right, a
frieze of small horses; to
the left a group of horses
and ibexes much distorted by
the angle of the camera.
Length of the cow 5 ft 8 ins.
See pp. 73–4.

Black horse superimposed on traces of red. In front of it a black sign in the shape of a cross is painted on a white stencilled ground. The horse is speckled with calcite flakes. Length 10 ft.
See page 76.

13

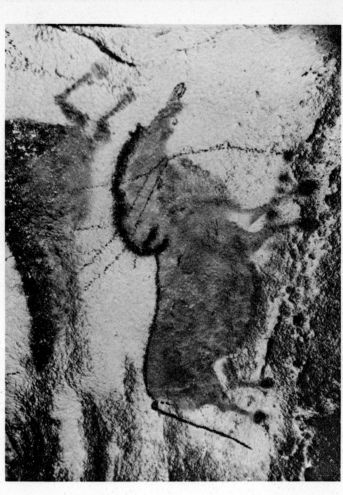

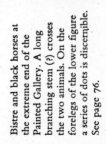

Bistre and black horses at
the extreme end of the
Painted Gallery. A long
branching stem (?) crosses
the two animals. On the
forelegs of the lower figure
a series of dots is discernible.
See page 76.

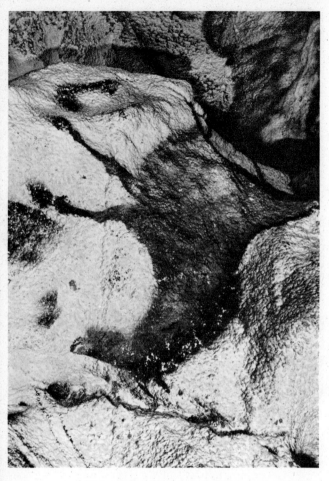

Bistre and black horse at the extreme end of the Painted Gallery belonging to the same group as the horses on Plate 14. To the left near the bottom of the plate another branching stem (?) can be seen. Here and there the body of the horse is speckled with a few calcite flakes. The animal is portrayed falling backwards and the painting is continued on the other side of the rock. In the lower right-hand corner a horse in red bands (Plate 16) – very distorted by the angle of the camera – is seen coming out of the tunnel.

See pp. 77 and 78.

15

Bison in red bands emerging from the tunnel at the end of the Painted Gallery followed by a horse of the same technique (lower right-hand corner of Plate 15). The figure is distorted by the angle of the camera. The few calcite flakes are of later date than the painting. See pp. 78 – 9.

Bison in black modelled technique in the cave of Marcenac. Except for the tail, the attitude is very similar to that of the bison on Plate 16. See page 79.

17

Forequarters of large black bull in the Painted Gallery. Adjacent to its horns, the horns of an earlier bistre bovid are plainly visible, and on the neck the underlying shape of a red cow (see fig. 13). In front of the bull, a black triple-branched sign is superposed on a very faded bistre horse. See page 74.

a. Large red cow with black head on the left-hand wall of the Painted Gallery. Note the double dorsal line, the slenderness of the horns, and the tuft of hair on the brow. Length 9 ft 4 ins. See page 74.

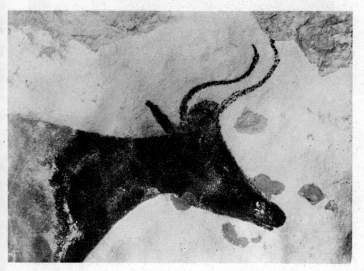

b. Detail of cow's head (Plate 19*a*). The flaking antedates the painting. See page 74.

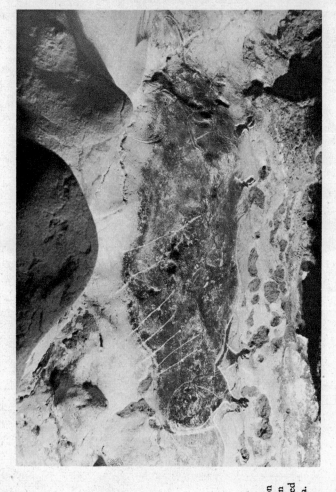

Painted and engraved bison at the entrance to the Main Gallery. It is much distorted by the angle of the camera. See Fig. 16 and page 88.

General view of the Main Gallery. At the top left-hand corner the cow with
the latticed signs and some horses; beyond, these figures, one of the two bison
depicted back to back. In the top right-hand corner the frieze of swimming
deer. In the background the start of the path leading to the Chamber of Felines.
See page 84.

Engraved head of deer in the Chamber of Engravings. The engraved line stands out white on older black paintings. Note the triangular mark on the neck. This may be a particular way of representing the second ear. See page 83.

Network of engravings on the walls of the small dome over the entrance to the Shaft of the Dead Man. In the lower centre a small cervid belonging to a frieze of three or four animals is clearly visible. Near the centre, a long almost horizontal natural vein in the rock is crossed by a multitude of small incised transverse strokes. At the very top, some polychrome latticed signs masked by a dark patch are barely discernible. See page 94.

Horse's head engraved on the wall of the Chamber of Engravings. Note the curious twisted perspective of the ears and the network of confused lines. See page 82.

Horse engraved on the walls of the Chamber of Engravings. The tail, the legs, and particularly the belly are very clear. It is associated with numerous signs. Within the belly a line ends in a cluster of diverging strokes reminiscent of the 'huts' or straw huts present in other caves, and on the hindquarters there is a geometric sign similar to the other latticed signs in the cave. See pp. 83 – 84.

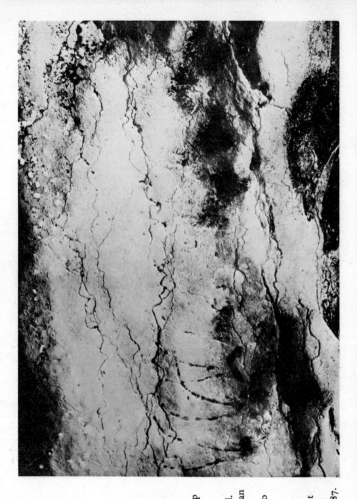

Frieze of ibexes heads. The left-hand group consists of four black heads with red horns; the right-hand group of three red heads, but the paint of the horns has almost completely vanished. An irregular latticed sign can be distinguished with difficulty between these two groups. A small head of some animal difficult to identify is superposed on the right-hand group, but it is not visible on the photograph. See Fig. 2 and page 87.

Detail of the preceding frieze (Plate 26) showing the left-hand group. Comparison of the two photographs is interesting. In the first, the lighting is directed on to the wall perpendicularly and the painting stands out. In the second, the lighting is softer and oblique and brings out the engraved lines and the reliefs. A few punctuations on the horns can still be distinguished, however.

a. Painted and engraved horse at the entrance to the Main Gallery. It is advancing towards a latticed sign painted in black. An arrow is engraved across its hind-quarters. Length 3 ft 8 ins. See Fig. 16 and page 87.

b. Painted and engraved horse from the large frieze of horses in the Main Gallery. A latticed sign is painted on the flank. See Plate 30 and page 89.

Detail of the back cow with latticed signs. Note the black line painted in front of the muzzle and compare with Plate 6. See pp. 88 – 9 and Plate 30.

General view of the large
frieze on the left-hand wall
of the Main Gallery. There
are three polychrome latticed
signs below the hindlegs and
the tail of the cow, but these
are not clearly visible on the
photograph.
See pp. 88 – 9.

30

Detail of the frieze of
Plate 30. Examined under a
magnifying glass several
details become apparent.
Note particularly the two
horses' heads emerging from
the hindquarters of the cow.
See pp. 88 – 9.

31

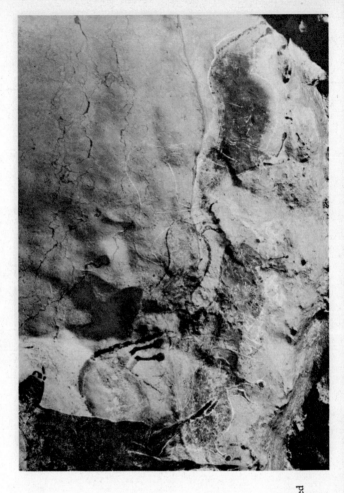

Another view of the frieze of horses of Plate 30. In the centre an unpainted engraved horse is very clear. See pp. 88 – 9.

Frieze of swimming deer in the Main Gallery. The neck of the second deer on the left shows the same peculiar feature as the engraved deer in Plate 22. The dark patch between the antlers of the third and fourth deer is the head and shoulders of a small bichrome horse in a poor state of preservation. Between the antlers of the fourth deer there is a series of punctuations. The fifth deer is brown, whereas all the others are black. Length of frieze 16 ft 8 ins.
See pp. 89–90.

33

One wall of the Chamber of Felines with three engraved felines and numerous signs. See Fig. 18 and page 91.

The scene in the Shaft of the Dead Man. The rhinoceros on the one hand and the wounded bison and the bird on the other were not executed in the same technique. See pp. 95–6.

35

Mammoths and bovids painted in black line in the cave of Pech-Merle at Cabrerets (Lot). See page 186.

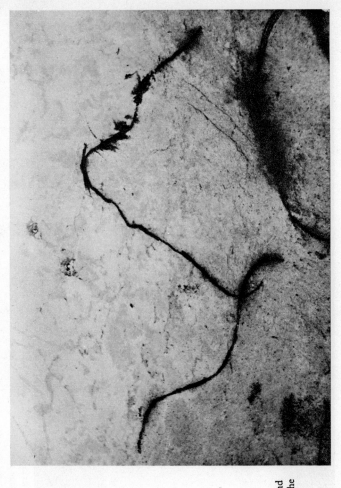

Sketch of a mammoth and
a bovid in black line in the
cave of Pech-Merle
Cabrerets (Lot)
See page 187.

37

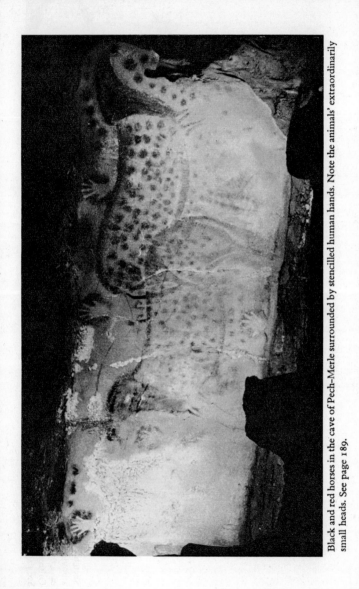

Black and red horses in the cave of Pech-Merle surrounded by stencilled human hands. Note the animals' extraordinarily small heads. See page 189.

Imaginary animals in the Gallery of Le Combel at Pech-Merle at Cabrerets (Lot). No real animal ever had such a globular body and tiny head. Note the strange composition of the three bodies, the first of which seems to have two heads and the last no head at all. See page 166.

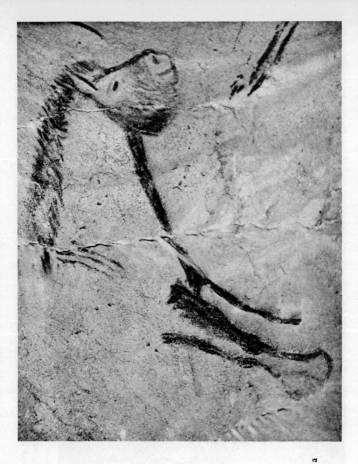

Small horse painted in black on a wall in the cave of Niaux. See page 129.

Two Bison back to back in the Main Gallery. The general symmetry, the movement of the hind-quarters, and the curves of the bellies proclaim the skill of the artist. Length of the group 8 ft. See page 89.

Detail of the frieze of
swimming deer. See
Plate 33 and page 90.

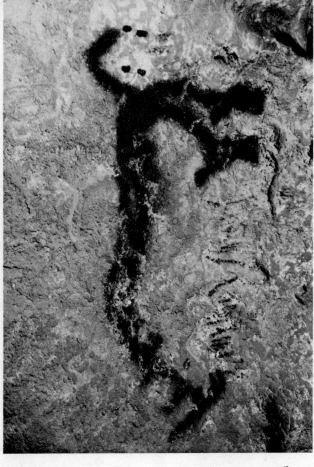

The rhinoceros in the Shaft of the Dead Man. It is modelled in black like the bulls in the Great Hall. The foreleg and the belly are merely sketched in.
The movement of the tail resembles that of the bison's tail on Plate 16.
See Plate 35 and page 95.

43

Venus of Laussel. This extraordinary low relief (Height 1 ft 6 ins) is of very different inspiration from the art of cave sanctuaries. See pp. 34 – 5.

Entrance to the Lascaux cave.

Equus caballus gmelini Antonius

The Tarpan, in the park-steppe of south Russia. This horse, which became extinct in 1851, was the western race of the wild horse, ranging from Turkestan to western Europe. It was not averse to forests, though open country was preferred, and it became the ancestor of all ordinary domestic breeds, including the Arab.

The Tarpan was more graceful than Przewalski's horse, and was mouse-grey, with a black upright mane continued by a stripe along the back to the tail. Some British ponies sometimes exhibit tarpan coloration.

Based on literary and pictorial evidence, and on 'reconstituted' specimens of Hellabrann Park, Munich. Painted by Miss M. Maitland Howard, under the direction of Professor F. E. Zeuner. See page 131.

Dicerorhinus merckii Jager

Merck's Rhinoceros at the Mousterian site of Ehringsdorf, near Weimar, central Germany. It is assumed that the rhinoceroses were caught in pits, and that young specimens were obtained more frequently than old ones. This is suggested by the proportions of the age classes composing the fossil material, as shown by Soergel. Ehringsdorf was a densely forested area of springs producing calcareous tufa in large quantities. The scene shows a mother and child approaching the water at night on a track across which a pit has been dug.

Painted by Miss M. Maitland Howard, under the direction of Professor F. E. Zeuner See pp. 146 – 8.

a. European Bison. See pp. 137 – 40

b. Bos primigenius. From a painting found in an Augsburg antique shop in 1827. See pp.133 – 7.

tried out in other painted caves, has not produced results of any interest. The best method is still a continual examination of the paintings in comparison with photographic records.

A distinction must be made between two kinds of super-position – superpositions dating from one and the same period, from which much can be learnt concerning the composition and meaning of the works, and successive superpositions, which disclose something of their evolution.

If two superposed figures are of the same style and form part of the same ensemble, the same group, or the same file of animals, they are of the same period. Such contemporaneous superpositions represent only one conception of composition, however; the composition is clearly deliberate when one figure partly covers another and the overlapping of the painted areas is inconsiderable. The last two bulls on the right of the Great Hall portrayed side by side, with the forelegs of one superposed on the flanks of the other, is an example of a skilful and deliberate composition, for the hindquarters of the bull on the second plane have not been depicted: the design was clearly conceived as a whole from its inception. Such effects, though easier to obtain in the case of figures rendered in line or in bands, are rarely seen in the paintings group, for the artist generally avoided superpositions by representing his animals one above the other without showing the extremities of the animal on the second plane (Plate 3).

Engraved superpositions are much clearer. It is probable that the large black cow in the Main Gallery is contemporary with the latticed sign accompanying it; and the underlying frieze of painted and engraved horses undoubtedly belongs to one single epoch, in spite of the intersection of several of the animals. Incised lines can be more easily superposed on each other without damage than layers of paint can, and there are two particularly striking instances of this kind of superposition in the Chamber of Engravings: the two deer confronting each other (Fig. 19), one partly superposed on the other without

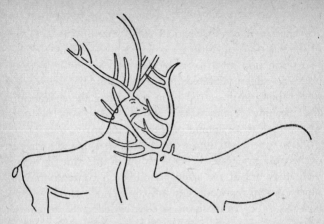

Fig. 19. Two deer facing each other engraved in the Chamber of Engravings.
Length of each figure about 10 inches.

detriment to either figure, and the file of small deer (Plate 23)
engraved above the mouth of the Shaft of the Dead Man.
These superpositions are contemporaneous, however, and can
give no clue to the chronology of the engravings. They should
be studied conjointly with the friezes and the scenes, particular
attention being paid to composition and meaning.

There are some paintings showing successive superpositions
at Lascaux, but in most cases the artists seem to have taken
pains to avoid destroying the general harmony of the cave
either by placing the new paintings so that they covered the
earlier ones as little as possible, or by attempting to obliterate
the earlier paintings completely. For example, the large black
bull of the Painted Gallery almost covers the whole of a frieze
of four heads of bistre-coloured bovids and two red cows, one
following the other (Plate 18 and Fig. 13). In other cases – the
bovids and the horses on the vault of the Painted Gallery, for
example (Plates 7 and 9) – deliberate arrangement is apparent,
so long as no attempt is made to fathom the general meaning
of any one of these paintings as a whole.

The different groups – the paintings, the engravings, and the combined paintings and engravings – should be studied separately. The figures in the paintings group can be classified without much difficulty according to the techniques employed. There are some exceptional figures in finely drawn line; other figures are outlined in wide bands and slightly modelled; others again are uniformly filled in with one colour – red, bistre, or black; and, lastly, certain figures are bichrome. There is only one instance of a polychrome figure. In many cases the bistre or red animals are encircled or re-touched with black, and they are the most difficult figures to study, because they could belong to two widely spaced periods. This brief classification might be complemented by a study of the various methods of applying the pigments. In some cases – for example, the bulls of the Great Hall or the rhinoceros in the Shaft (Plate 43) – the outline has been roughly sketched in a fine line which is still visible on the unfinished parts of the figure; in others the outline is indicated by a series of large dots. The bodies of the two ibexes confronting each other in the Painted Gallery are outlined in this way. Sometimes the two techniques are used jointly; the large-antlered deer (Plate 11) in this Gallery is depicted in this combined style. The particular manner of portraying a horse's mane with a fluffy effect is the most characteristic technique used in the Lascaux paintings.

It is clear that the black filling-in of animal figures is the most recent of the techniques mentioned. The black leaping cow (Plate 12) is superposed on a red patch which was probably an animal figure; as mentioned above, the large black bull in the Painted Gallery overlies a series of heads of bovids painted in bistre and two red cows (Fig. 13); and in the Great Hall of the Bulls a black horse with dappled filling-in is superposed on the imaginary animal and on one of the bulls painted in wide bands (Plate 1).

The bichrome animals, in bistre or red with extremities, head, and sometimes contours in black, cannot be attributed to this period or to a phase very close to it without some hesitation. Some of these animals have undoubtedly remained untouched since they were originally drawn; the horse of Plate 10 or the cow of Plate 9, for example, could not have been painted on two different occasions, for if the black outline of these figures is removed, only a meaningless patch of colour remains. In some instances, however, the second colour in the form of black re-touchings on red, bistre, or brown animal figures could have been added later. It is conceivable that some of the figures were painted at a particular period when bichrome painting was in fashion at Lascaux and that earlier figures were altered to conform to the prevailing taste. Many of the bichrome figures are horses, most of them in bistre, with fluffy mane. This mane undoubtedly belongs to one particular period late in the history of the cave, for only one is obliterated by other figures. At all events, from the attractive head and shoulders of the horse painted high on the walls of the Great Hall of the Bulls (Plate 1), it is clear that these manes are of later date than the large bulls painted in black bands and of earlier date than the frieze of swimming deer (Plate 33) painted over one of the five small fluffy-maned horses.

A clearly distinctive group, earlier than those mentioned above, consists of animals rendered in black bands and slightly modelled. The large bulls of the first chamber, the imaginary animal, the rhinoceros of the Shaft, are all examples of this technique. The three animals painted in red bands (Plate 16) emerging from the tunnel at the far end of the Painted Gallery may also belong to this group, but they cannot be included with certainty.

It is difficult to determine the exact chronological dating of the group. The figures are of earlier date than the black animals and the horses with fluffy manes and they may also be earlier than the red bovids with which they are intermingled. Although the red and black colours overlap to a great extent, it is not easy to determine which one underlies the other. According to Breuil, the black bulls may be the earliest figures. If a comparison is made between two photographs showing these superpositions in detail, one an ordinary monochrome photograph, the other infra-red, the black heads of the bulls stand out much more clearly from the red mass of the other bovids on the infra-red photograph than on the ordinary one.

In spite of the uncertainties, a study of the superpositions enables at least three phases of technique to be established at Lascaux without any comparisons being made with cave art elsewhere.* Apart from some unimportant vestiges and perhaps some bistre or red animals, the first and earliest phase is represented by:

> The three animals in red bands at the far end of the Painted Gallery (Plate 16).
> The two ibexes facing each other.
> The deer with enormous antlers (Plate 11).
> The four bistre heads of bovids emerging from the large black bull of the same Gallery may also date from the earliest frequentation of the cave.
> The black modelled animals (Plates 2, 5, 6, and 43).
> Probably certain animals in flat wash (red bovids, small deer, etc.).

The second phase is represented by:

> The bichrome animals (Plates 8, 9, 10, 14, and 15).
> The bistre horses with black manes.

---

* The classification of the paintings at Lascaux established by Abbé Breuil consists of fourteen series. It is based not only on the superpositions, which cannot be described in detail here, but also on comparisons with other caves. A small brown deer encircled with black is partially covered by one of the bulls of the Great Hall. Its technique relates it to one of the horses of the Painted Gallery – light bistre, encircled with black – and the two paintings probably belong to the same period. If this deduction is correct, the bichrome technique must have been used both before and after the period of the large bulls rendered in black bands and lightly modelled, and this may considerably narrow the gap between the dates of the different works at Lascaux.

The red bovids accentuated with black.

This group may includes the true bichrome paintings and earlier figures re-touched with black.

The third phase is represented by:

Animals filled in entirely in black (Plates 12, 13, and 18).

In the Painted Galleries there are no superpositions of bichrome phase and entirely black phase, but their order of succession can be checked by comparison with the painted and engraved figures in the Main Gallery. The parallelism is somewhat difficult to establish, but if it is accepted that the technique of engraving does not constitute a stage of artistic development and is essentially dependent on the nature of the walls, a link with the painted works can reasonably be established. The large cow painted in flat black wash with an incised outline which is the central subject on the left-hand wall in the Main Gallery (Plates 29 and 30), is probably contemporaneous with the large black bovids in other parts of the cave (Phase 3). There are also black-painted animals of similar technique, but much effaced, in the Chamber of Engravings and they are earlier than the numerous engravings superposed on them. Conversely, the large cow with the latticed signs is of later date than the magnificent frieze of horses covering most of the wall (Plates 28b, 29, 30, 31, and 32). The paint of these horses is likewise much effaced, but their bristling manes undoubtedly relate them to the bistre and black horses with fluffy manes (Phase 2).

Finally, the following sequence of superpositions can be considered as established for the cave as a whole except for any corrections of detail which may become necessary at a later date. The latest designs are the fine intersecting engravings in the Chamber of Engravings (Phase 4; Plates 22, 23, 24, and 25). When they were executed, the decoration of the cave was already more or less as it is today. The large black bovids of the two Galleries – majestic, isolated, each massive body dominating one entire wall – were painted in the preceding period (Phase 3). The earlier history of the cave is more difficult to reconstruct. There were at least two phases: the phase of the bichrome animals (Phase 2) with its chains of bristling-maned horses, and a phase whose masterpiece is the frieze of large black bulls outlined in black bands and slightly modelled (Phase 1).

The Evolution of the Various Styles and the Duration of the Cave's Use

The study of the archaeological evidence at Lascaux suggests an occupation date of about 13,000 years B.C.; the study of the paintings enables the decoration of the cave to be placed in the second half of Breuil's Aurignacio-Perigordian cycle; and a study of the evolution of the techniques, styles, and subjects gives an indication of the length of time between the execution of the first paintings and the final abandonment of the cave. Generally speaking, very marked differences between the first and last works would seem to imply that there was a long interval between them, and great homogeneity that the frequentation of the cave was of very short duration. In no circumstances is it possible to go beyond these general conclusions or to lay down any specific time limits.

The continuous sequence of the superpositions has been determined by a study of the differences in technique between each particular group of figures. These differences are very clear. They are apparent both in the method of applying the paint and in the colours used. Without describing in detail the application of the paint – whether it was applied with the fingers or with a brush – or the various processes used from the sketch to the finished work, one fact stands out clearly – the artists of Lascaux knew of and used a process rarely employed in other painted caves: they were able to produce a blurred effect for a contour or a filling-in and use it in conjunction with clear and precise brush-strokes. This technique was used especially for depicting horses' manes (Plate 10), but it is apparent that certain details of the animal figures painted in black bands in modelled technique could hardly have been produced by means of a mere brush (Plate 6). Nothing is known of the actual process, but it is believed to have consisted of a technique of applying powdered pigment by means of a primitive type of spray gun. The important fact is that this manner of depicting horses' manes is found especially at Lascaux, whereas the black modelled technique has been used in several caves. The great majority of the horses at Lascaux have been painted with this blurred effect.

The other methods – the drawing of silhouettes in line, the use of dots to mark the contours of a body, and a form of dappling for filling-in, the painting of animals in wide bands, with or without a modelled effect, the filling-in of silhouettes in flat wash – are very varied and would seem to imply great technical changes from one period to another. The sequence of these techniques at Lascaux is not sufficiently clearly established, however, for any definite conclusions to be drawn. For example, dots are used in the representation of the two ibexes facing each other, which are generally considered to be of early date, as well as in the excellent rendering of one of the bistre-and-black horses of the vault.

The colours vary from group to group: sometimes one colour seems to have been more in favour than another. These preferences may have been due to the need for an economical use of some raw material which was particularly prized and difficult to obtain; or they may have been inspired by religious faith – by the belief in the greater efficacy of a certain red, or a particularly intense black, for example; or they may have been merely the result of a change in aesthetic taste. Whatever the reason, two of the three pictorial phases described above are monochrome, with in between them a bichrome phase during which black was used only to intensify the effect of the bistre or the reds.

It is not known how these variations of colours or techniques on which the sequence of the superpositions has been based are to be interpreted in terms of time. Were they due to a slow evolution, or to a desire for change or novelty, or to the need to express something new in a different manner? The answer is unknown.

Variations in style may perhaps prove to be more revealing than changes in technique, because in principle they are made unintentionally or unconsciously, and style conforms to tradition, with which it is not easy to break. One of the most characteristic stylistic features, and one of the easiest to isolate, is the manner of representing the hoofs, horns or antlers, and ears of bovids and cervids. The blank spaces or white lines in the filling-in of animals which mark a joint or outline a limb are also characteristic of a great many figures at Lascaux.

The hoofs of most of the bovids are depicted in a very distinctive manner: the two divisions of the cloven hoof are shown frontally, whereas the leg and thigh are shown in profile (Plate 18). Sometimes the two dewclaws are depicted also, one placed above the other (Plate 20). This conception of perspective is the 'twisted perspective' of Abbé Breuil. It would be interesting to determine whether this 'twisted perspective' is confined to one period at Lascaux, or whether it evolved gradually as different groups of paintings succeeded each other.

'Twisted perspective' is not used exclusively, however. An inventory of the feet of the bovids in the cave shows three different ways of depicting them (Fig. 20). The most characteristic and frequent manner of representing the extremity of a limb was to show it as two elongated and parallel ovals separated by a wide cleft; the ovals represent the hoof divisions, which are almost always asymmetrical. Generally, one dewclaw is shown, but sometimes two are depicted. There are some instances of an approximation to a true profile outline, but an absolute profile was never achieved. The extremities of many figures are either incomplete or non-existent (Plate 19).

In the group of animals painted in slightly modelled black or red bands, all three forms are present. Incomplete extremities are numerous: sometimes they are represented by a shapeless thickening of the limb; sometimes, on the contrary, the limb is gradually thinned until it fades into nothing; and occasionally it is depicted by a dead-straight line. Forked extremities also occur. There are no examples of hoofs shown in almost normal perspective; the others are in typical 'twisted perspective'. The extremities of the bison painted in red bands (Plate 16) are merely rounded ends to the limbs; those of the bison in the Shaft, which cannot be ascribed to the period of painting in modelled technique with any certainty, show three forms: two extremities are in 'twisted perspective', one is incomplete, and one is forked (Plate 35 and Fig. 20c). The bulls in the Great Hall (Fig. 20j) show in all six extremities in 'twisted perspective', two of indeterminate type, two incomplete, and one forked. If the two bison, which may belong to the same period – the bison painted in red bands at the far end of the Painted Gallery, and the wounded bison of the Shaft – are included, the total number of hoofs in 'twisted perspective' amounts to eight, as against seven indeterminate and two forked types (Fig. 20c and j) and two which resemble a hoof in almost normal perspective (Fig. 20j).

In the group of red bovids, both with and without black retouchings, the comparative numbers of the various types of extremity are slightly different. In the Great Hall of the Bulls there are three examples of extremities in 'twisted perspective' as against five indeterminate types (Fig. 20g); under the large black bull there is one example of 'twisted perspective' as against four indeterminate types (Plate 18 and Fig. 13). The artist never took the trouble to depict the four extremities of the cow with the black collarette clearly (Fig. 20h) and they

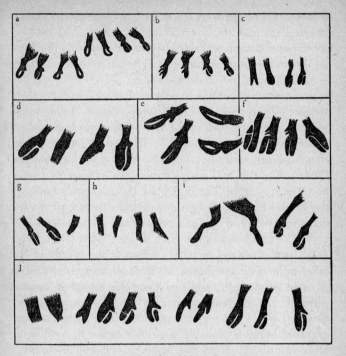

Fig. 20. Examples of bovids' hoofs at Lascaux:

Bison.
    (*a*) The bison depicted back to back (Plate 43).
    (*b*) The painted and engraved bison of Fig. 16.
    (*c*) The bison in the Shaft (Plate 37).

Bovids painted in plain black.
    (*d*) The large black bull in the Painted Gallery (Plate 18).
    (*e*) The leaping cow (Plate 12).
    (*f*) The cow associated with latticed signs (Plate 32).

Bovids painted in red or red and black.
    (*g*) Red bovid of Fig. 10.
    (*h*) Cow with black head in the Painted Gallery (Plate 19).
    (*i*) Cows on the vault of the Painted Gallery (Plates 8 and 9).

Bulls in slightly modelled black bands.
    (*j*) The bulls of the Great Hall (Plate 1).

fade into the cornice. Very few of the legs of the red-and-black bovids of the vault are shown (Plates 7, 9, and Fig. 20*i*), but two are depicted in unmistakable 'twisted perspective'. (Six legs are shown for a total of three animal figures, two of which are much obliterated and undecipherable.)

In the group of animals filled in with black, the extremities are carefully represented, and the proportion in 'twisted perspective' is higher. Each of the four hoofs of the leaping cow (Plate 12 and Fig. 20*e*) seems to show two divisions. The elongated form of the hoofs of the cow with the latticed signs (Plate 30 and Fig. 20*f*) bears a curious resemblance to the extremities of a cervid. The large black bull is the only figure in the series which shows two incomplete extremities; the remaining two are in 'twisted perspective' (Plate 18 and Fig. 20*d*). The two bison shown back to back (Plate 41 and Fig. 21*a*) Breuil attributes to a later period in the history of the cave; eight hoofs are shown, seven of which are depicted in 'twisted perspective', and one resembles a hoof in normal perspective. One bison painted in reddish-brown and engraved (Figs. 16 and 20*b*) and associated with the painted and engraved horses is probably somewhat earlier than the large black animals; it shows two hoofs in 'twisted perspective' and two, which are less clear, with the two dewclaws (Fig. 17).

The use of normal perspective in the representation of the hoofs of bovids is practically unknown at Lascaux. The characteristic representation is in 'twisted perspective' attenuated by the asymmetry of the dewclaws, and this method has likewise been used in other Palaeolithic caves – at Font-de-Gaume, for example, and Altamira. Incomplete extremities are rare in the latest group.

The hoofs of cervids are rendered according to the same convention, except that the two ovals which represent the two divisions of the cloven hoof are more elongated, and the trend of development seems to be similar. The earliest group in the

Great Hall of the Bulls shows some incomplete extremities, whereas the slender legs of the deer in the Chamber of Engravings, which are undoubtedly of later date, end in elongated hoofs with the two ovals carefully painted and engraved.

Somewhat different results are obtained from a study of the horns. From the earliest to the latest phases, greater homogeneity is shown. A typical 'twisted perspective' is the representation of the two horns springing symmetrically from both sides of the forehead in the shape of a somewhat distorted lyre. In fact, this method is rarely applied absolutely at Lascaux; the 'twisted perspective' is nearly always attenuated, the lyre shape asymmetrical, and the two horns tend to be shown parallel to each other. They are completely parallel on a large number of figures, but there are many variations of these two conventions. In certain of the more evolved figures, one horn only is shown, but there are no instances of true Magdalenian perspective where one horn conceals part of the other (Fig. 21).

The antlers of deer are depicted according to the same principle, and in their case the true 'twisted perspective' whereby two antlers are shown symmetrically in relation to the centre of the forehead is never used. The two antlers diverge from a single frontal point: one is almost vertical, the other thrown back in order to leave the necessary space for the frontal tines and avoid superposing them on those of the other antler. This method is systematically used and the angle of the antlers provides its only variation (Figs. 22 and 23).

The ears of both bovids and cervids at Lascaux are represented in a very homogeneous and rather surprising manner – indeed, at first sight there is some doubt whether they are in fact ears. In the paintings of the Great Hall of the Bulls, as well as in the later works of the two Galleries, ears are represented by a thick, vertical line which appears to be placed slightly behind the base of the horns or the antlers (Plates 5 and 6).

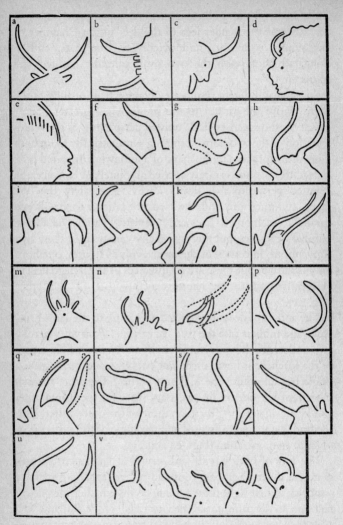

Fig. 21. Examples of bovids' horns at Lascaux. For key see opposite page.

These ears might be described as 'dagger-shaped', and they are shown singly * in a manner which is a sort of attenuated 'twisted perspective'. In fact, if the head were drawn full face on a profiled body, one ear would be shown on each side of the horns or antlers. The only two examples at Lascaux of this type are covered by the large black bull in the Painted

* One of the engraved deer in the Chamber of Engravings (Plate 23 and Fig. 22*h*) and two or perhaps three of the frieze of swimming deer show a curious elongated triangular design on the neck which may perhaps symbolize the second ear (Plate 42 and Fig. 23). To the knowledge of the writer there is nothing analogous in cave art elsewhere. It probably indicates that the two works are contemporaneous.

Key to Fig. 21:

Bison.
  (*a*) Bison's head engraved in the Lateral Passage.
  (*b*) Bison in the Shaft of the Dead Man (Plate 35).
  (*c*) Painted and engraved bison in the Main Gallery (Fig. 16). Other engraved horns would seem to indicate that several heads of the same bison were superposed one on the other.
  (*d* and *e*) The two bison depicted back to back (Plate 41).

Bovids painted in plain black.
  (*f*) The large black bull in the Painted Gallery (Plate 18).
  (*g*) The leaping cow (Plate 12).
  (*h*) The cow associated with latticed signs (Plate 29).

The red and black bovids of the Painted Gallery.
  (*i, j,* and *k*) Bovids on the vault (Plates 7 and 9).
  (*l*) Cow with black head (Plate 19).

Red bovids.
  (*m* and *n*) Bovids underlying the large black bull in the Painted Gallery. These are the only figures at Lascaux showing both ears (Fig. 13).
  (*o*) Bovid of Fig. 11. (Additional pair of black horns shown in dotted line.)
  (*p*) Bovid of Fig. 10.

Bulls in slightly modelled block bands.
  (*q*) First bull on the left. Underlying red outline in dotted line (Plate 1).
  (*r, s,* and *t*) Second, third, and fourth bulls.

Bull in black or bistre line sketched on the ceiling of the Painted Gallery.
  (*u*) This figure is very like the Bulls of the Great Hall, but its ear has not been depicted.
  (*v*) Heads of bistre bovids underlying the large black bull in the Painted Gallery (cf. Fig. 13).

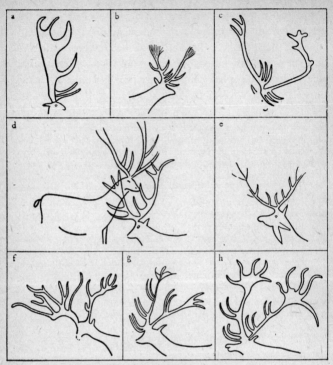

Fig. 22. Examples of cervids' antlers and ears at Lascaux.

(a) Head of a deer engraved in the Chamber of Engravings.
(b) Small painted deer in the Great Hall of the Bulls.
(c) Painted and engraved deer in the Chamber of Engravings (cf. Fig. 14).
(d) Deer facing each other engraved in the Chamber of Engravings.
(e) Engraved deer in the Chamber of Engravings (Plate 23).
(f and g) Painted deer in the Great Hall of the Bulls (Plate 4).
(h) Large deer in the Great Hall of the Bulls (Plate 11).

Gallery (see Figs. 13 and 21 (m and n)). Ears are represented in this dagger shape in all the various groups of technique used at Lascaux, and this or similar methods of portraying them is not unknown in other Palaeolithic caves (Altamira, Font-de-Gaume, Ebbou, Gargas, etc.), but nowhere has it been so systematically applied as at Lascaux.

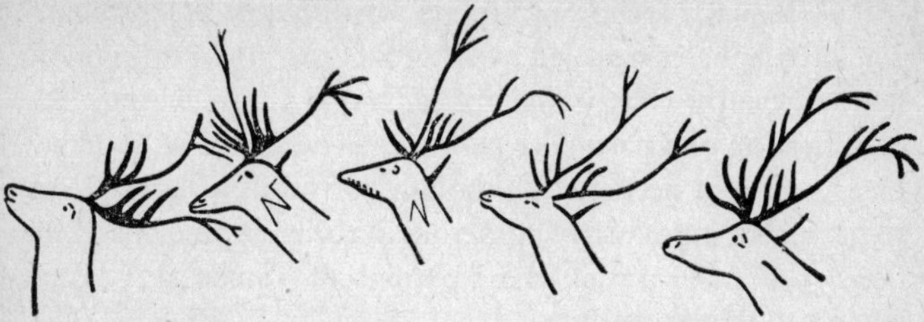

Fig. 23. Examples of cervids' antlers and ears at Lascaux. The frieze of swimming deer (Plates 33 and 42). The necks of several of the figures show a mark identical with that on the deer of Plate 22. These marks are probably an unusual way of showing the two ears.

Another very characteristic feature of Lascaux is the utilization of blank areas in the form of lines and spaces to give an effect of relief or to emphasize the details of a figure. This method has been used in each of the various groups of technique (animals in black modelled effect, in flat red or bistre wash, in bichrome and in flat black wash) for the portrayal of all species (horses, bovids, cervids, etc.). In the engraved series less use is made of it because it is replaced by incisions which stand out clearly against the background, generally painted, and serve the same purpose. Nevertheless, these blank spaces have been left in the bellies of most of the painted and engraved horses. In the group of paintings, these spaces have principally been used to indicate the bellies of animals (bistre and black horse of the Painted Gallery, Plate 10) and the interior of the thighs (the rhinoceros, Plate 43), or to mark the overlapping of a pair of legs which would otherwise be merged in one single patch of colour (the leaping cow, Plate 12). The details of the nostrils, the lips, or the eye are likewise often indicated by spaces left blank or made by scraping off the paint (the bulls of the Great Hall, the black bull of the Painted Gallery, Plates 6 and 18). Examples almost as numerous as the animal paintings themselves could be cited.

At Lascaux and in the majority of decorated caves the

species depicted are few: oxen, horses, and deer predominate. The broad phases revealed by a study of the superpositions are not sufficiently clearly established, however, to warrant the classification of a particular period as a 'period of wild oxen', or a 'period of deer', etc., although portrayals of horses seem to have been particularly numerous in the bichrome phase: indeed, the majority of the paintings of equids at Lascaux belong to this phase.

The signs accompanying the animals can be divided into definite periods; their number undoubtedly increases in the later phases. In the Great Hall of the Bulls punctuations accompany the early figures; in the Painted Gallery they are clearly connected with a bichrome horse; and in the Main Gallery they are associated with the antlers of a deer. Painted darts are not very numerous except in the group of red-and-black bovids, and among the bistre-and-black horses in the Painted Gallery (Plates 7, 9, and 10); engraved darts are much more abundant (Plate 28b). The harpoons incised on the walls of the Chamber of Engravings probably belong to the latest period of the engravings.

The number of the latticed signs (Fig. 25) so characteristic of Lascaux likewise increases in the last phase of the cave's use. There is none in the Great Hall and there are only four in the Painted Gallery. One is a rough sketch – a mere rectangle outlined under the deer with the large antlers (Plate 11) – and another is placed between the two ibexes facing each other, which are situated at the far end of the Gallery. The age of these figures is somewhat uncertain. The third sign, the 'hurdle' over which the leaping cow seems about to jump (Plate 12), belongs to the phase of the large black animals in flat wash. There is also a sign of similar type on the vault between the red bovids and the bichrome horses. The remaining latticed signs – about thirty in all – are engraved, or painted and engraved, in the Main Gallery (Plates 28a, 28b, 30, and 31), in the Chamber of Engravings (Plate 25), and in the

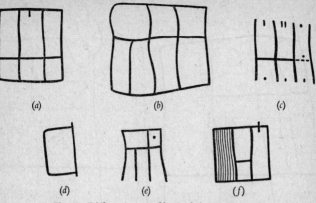

Fig. 24. Different types of latticed sign at Lascaux.

(a) Sign painted in red separating the two ibexes on the right-hand wall of the Painted Gallery.
(b) Large sign painted in red-brown in front of the leaping cow (Plate 12).
(c) Sign painted in black in front of the horse of Fig. 16.
(d) Sign painted in black in front of the large deer in the Great Hall of the Bulls (Plate 11).
(e) Sign painted in red on the ceiling of the Painted Gallery (Plate 7).
(f) Engraved sign in the Chamber of Felines.

Chamber of Felines (Plate 34). They belong to the last periods of the cave's frequentation (the period of the painted and engraved horses, the black bovids, and the engravings). The latticed signs below the feet of the large black cow are finely engraved and painted in several colours (Fig. 25). Identical polychrome signs appear in the Chamber of Engravings immediately above the mouth of the Shaft. These signs are accompanied by numerous engraved lines, but are not masked by them, which indicates that, at the period when the Chamber of Engravings was covered with its countless engraved figures, the polychrome chequerboards still had some significance for the last artists of the cave. Perhaps the period of the large animal paintings in flat black wash was then not far distant.

*

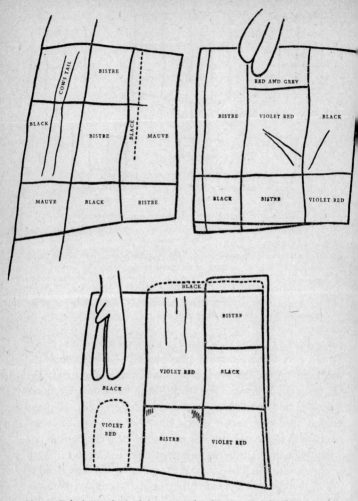

Fig. 25. Polychrome latticed signs painted and engraved under the extremities and the tail of the black cow in the Main Gallery (see Plates 30 and 31). The dotted lines indicate the areas of paint not defined by an engraved line. The double lines represent two incised lines.

The paintings and engravings at Lascaux are thus seen to be both diverse and homogeneous, and it is difficult to strike a balance between these two aspects. Homogeneous as they are in style, in a certain manner of representing the legs, horns, ears, and nostrils, there were nevertheless distinct stages during the course of which variations occurred in techniques and in the representation of objects or signs of human invention.

It is generally accepted that certain Palaeolithic caves were used continuously over very long periods of time, which possibly amounted to several millennia. Such a conclusion seems hardly admissible as far as Lascaux is concerned, however, for it differs greatly from other caves in the region and must be considered as a whole – a unity – with many characteristics peculiar to itself repeated exactly from one end of the cave to the other, and with paintings in a uniform state of preservation.* It is difficult to imagine how the art of this cave situated at the centre of a region of vigorous artistic culture could have developed gradually over a very long period and still have retained its individual characteristics. It seems legitimate to accept the theory that the most important period of the frequentation of Lascaux was of comparatively limited duration – perhaps about 1,000 years.

* Those in the poorest state of preservation are the black paintings in the Chamber of Engravings, which are undoubtedly of later date.

CHAPTER 3

THE EXTINCT FAUNA

THE study of the fauna depicted in a cave consists basically in the compiling of inventories and comparative lists of identification – inventories of the species represented and identification by comparison with fossil species and existing wild species. Such lists and inventories provide a double source of information about the actual animals which the cave artists knew and hunted, and, in addition, the climate and the environment in which they lived. Comparison with the bones found in archaeological levels likewise enables the age attributed to the different stylistic groups of the cave to be verified and determined, albeit to a limited extent. Unfortunately, the number of species depicted on the walls does not necessarily bear any relation to the actual number living at that time. The one indisputable fact – proved by the verisimilitude of the representations – is that all the animals painted or engraved at Lascaux were animals actually living and seen there. The frequency of their appearance on the walls is no guarantee of their prevalence at that period in the valley of the Vézère, however, nor does their absence mean that they were extinct by that time. The choice of subject may have been dependent on numerous factors – psychological, magical, or religious – which cannot be explained so long as the purpose of the underground sanctuaries is unknown.

As the inventory of the engravings at Lascaux is not yet completed, the numbers cited here for each species can only be approximate. On the one hand, they include all the painted figures; on the other, only the most important of the painted and engraved figures and of those which are engraved only; therefore the total number is smaller than the sum total of the figures portrayed in the cave. The relative proportion of each species listed in a complete inventory however would doubtless differ only to a very slight degree from the figures submitted here.

The species most frequently represented at Lascaux is the horse, of which there are more than one hundred portrayals; next come the bovids with thirty portrayals, followed by at least twenty deer, ten ibexes, excluding all the small engraved silhouettes in the Lateral Passage or in the Chamber of Engravings, then seven bison and six or seven felines. Certain species are represented by one figure only – for example, the bear, the musk-ox, and the reindeer. There is also only one painted rhinoceros, although there appears to be one other portrayal of this animal, but it is incomplete, in the series of engravings. It would seem inappropriate to include the imaginary animal at the entrance of the cave in a study of the fauna.

THE EQUIDS

The greater part of the very large number of horses portrayed at Lascaux seems to belong to a late phase – about the second half of the period of the cave's decoration. In the painted chambers particularly, the horses depicted are principally bichrome animals with black fluffy manes; in the engraved chambers they are painted and engraved, their manes accentuated by a series of fine parallel hatchings. Some of them underlie the large black cow in the Main Gallery.

The great number of horse portrayals cannot be regarded as an indication of any particular archaeological period; portrayal of the horse was widespread during the Upper Palaeolithic and began to decrease only in evolved Magdalenian sites. Horses were indeed particularly abundant in the region of the Vézère at the beginning of the Magdalenian, but it must be emphasized that there is no evidence to prove that the artists were particularly inspired by those species which were most numerous. Indeed, the contrary is just as likely. If, as is often supposed, animal representations were used as a means of ensuring the success of the hunt, magic rites might rather have been used to ensnare rarer animals, more difficult to hunt. The discovery of fragments of horse-bones in the hearth beyond the Chamber of Felines merely proves that the horse was undoubtedly regarded as game (and not as a taboo animal) by the men who frequented Lascaux; and, as it is impossible to state precisely to what period of the cave's use the hearth belongs, this discovery is of little value as chronological evidence.

A great many of the horses at Lascaux display characteristics which are both striking and homogeneous. Their swollen bodies, ridiculously short limbs, and small elongated heads give them a very grotesque appearance bearing little resemblance to the types living today. Horses showing these characteristics are of frequent occurrence in Palaeolithic cave art; the microcephalic horses of Pech-Merle (Plate 38), the 'duck-bill' horses in the cave of Le Portel in the Pyrenees, the horses at Pair-non-Pair, Altamira, and some other sites bear a striking resemblance to those at Lascaux (Fig. 26). These animals with

Fig. 26. Examples of horses with tapering or 'duck-bill' heads in the caves of Lascaux, Pech-Merle, and Le Portel.

slim tapering head under an enormous mane, and massive body on over-short legs are in fact found in many deep caves. In others, on the contrary, the type represented is closer to the horse of today: the head is larger and thicker, the legs longer. The horses of Les Combarelles, a black horse in modelled technique at Font-de-Gaume, the horses of the later series at Altamira, and the engraved horses of Teyjat are of this type, of which the most charming example is the little bearded horse at Niaux.

Since none of the representations can be confidently dated it is difficult to give a detailed chronological classification of the two types. Generally speaking, the elongated heads belong to an earlier period of cave art, while the thicker, squatter heads belong to a more or less evolved Magdalenian period. It is not easy to determine whether the artists were inspired by a change of type in the living model, or whether the difference in the representations was due to an evolution in style, and the palaeontological evidence for the very short span of the Upper Palaeolithic is insufficient to provide any solution to the problem.*

At Lascaux, the proportions of the head vary from one figure to another. The little horses painted below the leaping cow have short, stocky bodies with massive heads (Plate 12); the black horse with three legs (Fig. 12) at the entrance to the Painted Gallery is an example of the type with elongated head; and there are many examples of variations between the two extremes. These variations may be the result of inaccurate representation by the Quaternary artists, or of a desire to produce a particular stylistic effect; or such variations in type may

---

* For information on Quaternary horses see E. Bourdelle, 'Essai d'une étude morphologique des équidés préhistoriques de France, d'après les gravures rupestres', *Mammalia*, Vol. II, 1938, p. 1; E. Bourdelle, 'Les équidés préhistoriques représentés par les dessins et sculptures rupestres des grottes des Eyzies (Dordogne)', *Bull. de la Société d'Acclimatation*, 1933, p. 461; E. Bourdelle et F. Trombe, 'Les dessins d'équidés préhistoriques de Ganties-Montespan (Haute-Garonne)', *Mammalia*, Vol. X, 1946, p. 13.

Fig. 27. Horse at Le Portel showing an almost schematic pattern
of coat and mane.

in fact have been seen by the artists during the course of hunting expeditions and then reproduced by them – perhaps with some exaggeration – on the walls of the caves. It is possible also that the true red colour of the large bichrome horse in the Great Hall of the Bulls (Plate 3) and the two horses in the tunnel does in fact portray a different variety of coat.

There are also other features which are puzzling and difficult to interpret. For example, at the base of the mane on certain painted horses a series of two, three, or four parallel strokes, somewhat difficult to distinguish from the mane itself, is often present, though sometimes these strokes are very clearly defined (Plate 14). Similar strokes are apparent on certain engraved animals (they are very clear on Plate 32, for example), which proves that they do not represent a special manner of painting horses' manes. There is, moreover, no likelihood of their being due to the personal fancy of the individual artists of Lascaux, for they are found in caves as diverse as Niaux, Le Gabillou, and Arcy-sur-Cure, and they are very evident on the majority of the horses of Le Portel (Fig. 25).* It is impossible to determine whether these strokes portray a special feature of the coat of prehistoric horses, or represent one of the signs whose meaning is still obscure,† though this is less likely.

The belly of most of the figures is so swollen that the animals are described as pregnant females. The male organ is scarcely ever indicated; a stallion pierced by seven darts, which is part of an engraved group at the entrance to the Main Gallery, and one of the bichrome horses of the Painted Gallery would seem to be exceptions, but these figures are not at all clear. A hairless tail is often represented by one single line of paint, or by a double incision of the burin; but sometimes the tail is thicker and has the tufted appearance of the tails of wild horses. The ears are generally represented in 'twisted perspective'. A bistre animal with an enormous belly and a long thin tail has elongated ears reminiscent of those of a wild ass (Fig. 28), and it is associated with another animal of similar technique which is undoubtedly of the same species, though it is not very clear.

Apart from these figures, the equids would seem to be represented by a somewhat variable type of wild horse with a small head and a heavy body. According to palaeontological evidence,‡ Quaternary equids, apart from a few asses, varied little in shape from a common type with a broad head and stocky limbs. There is only one type of wild horse in the world today – the Przewalski horse, whose habitat is the steppes of Mongolia – although another type of horse, the Tarpan, lived in a wild state in the steppes of Southern Russia until recently.

---

* There is an evident relationship between the horses of Lascaux and those of Le Portel. The shape of the head, the short legs, the swollen body, the tapering tail are present in both caves. Even the manner of representing the head and shoulders of a horse with a fluffy mane which prevailed for a time at Lascaux spread as far as Le Portel.

† Perhaps they represent a marking of the coat similar to the cross on an ass's back which the domestic horse must have lost.

‡ M. Boule and J. Piveteau, *Les Fossiles*, 1955, p. 651.

Fig. 28. Wild ass at Lascaux.

The description of the wild horse of today tallies strikingly with the characteristics of the painted horses at Lascaux. It is smaller than the domestic horse, very sturdy, with a large drooping belly and short limbs, and the details of its colouring are faithfully reproduced on some of the Lascaux animals. Its mane is black, short, and stands straight up instead of falling to the side like that of the domestic horse. The blurred outlines of the manes on the paintings and the hatched lines on the engravings are undoubtedly exact representations of characteristics of the real animals of prehistoric times. The body of the wild horse is lighter in colour than the mane and the belly is almost white. It would seem to be almost identical in type with the little bistre, white, and black horse of Plate 10, except that the squat head of the Przewalski horse bears no resemblance to the heads portrayed at Lascaux. Professor Bourdelle points out, however, that in a collection of Przewalski horse bones belonging to the Musée d'Histoire Naturelle de Paris there was great variation in the size and shape of the heads: some were massive and down-curved, others small with a flattened profile.* At Lascaux this curious disproportion of the head in

* Bourdelle, the articles quoted, and Robert Hainard, *Les Mammifères sauvages d'Europe*, 1949, II, p. 206.

relation to the rest of the body may represent an exaggeration of a characteristic actually observed.

Other varieties of wild horses existed elsewhere in Europe until a comparatively short time ago.* It is not known in every case whether they were of ancient stock or descended from domestic escapes which had reverted to a wild state. The wild horse of the Alps mentioned by Strabo, which was grey, with a dark dorsal line, survived until the fifteenth century. At the end of the sixteenth century, wild horses were abundant in the Vosges, in Prussia, and in Lithuania; in the eighteenth century they were found in the famous forest of Bielowitza, the hunting-ground of the Polish kings; and in the nineteenth century they existed only on the steppes of Southern Russia.

Some details of these animals are known from accounts of ancient writers. Unfortunately, these always refer to beasts which were hunted by man to a greater or lesser extent and gradually driven back as cultivation of the land increased; so their habitat in historic times is not necessarily their natural home. The wild horse of Russia inhabited the steppe, where the Przewalski horse is found today, and other European wild horses lived principally in forests, where they fed on broom, heather, and leaves. These facts prove at least that horses could adapt themselves to life in the forest or on the steppe-land and to cold or temperate conditions, but never to a completely glacial climate.

THE OX-TRIBE

Bovids are the most impressive animal figures at Lascaux, both by reason of their size and because of their dominant place among the other animals. They belong principally to the various series of paintings – each style includes some portrayals of them. They are found in the earliest series – for example, the frieze of bistre horned heads emerging from the back of the large black bull, the figures in plain

* *Les Mammifères sauvages d'Europe*, 'Les équidés', pp. 205-8.

red colour, and the bulls in black bands and modelled technique of the Great Hall – and in the bichrome series in which they are represented by the red-and-black cows of the Painted Gallery. They are also the most characteristic of the large animals painted in flat black wash. There are a few examples in the engravings in the Lateral Passage and in the Chamber of Engravings, however, both with and without traces of paint. These large numbers are exceptional in cave art, for the percentage of oxen in the fauna portrayed is usually small. Nevertheless, some examples are found in most caves: Altamira, Font-de-Gaume, Les Combarelles, La Mouthe, Pech-Merle, Le Portel, Teyjat, etc.

The Lascaux oxen are of two very distinct types – one a massive animal, the other of slighter build. Until very recently it was generally considered that the massive type represented the *Bos primigenius* found in the Quaternary sites of Europe, and the slighter form the *Bos longifrons*, considerably different in type and of smaller size. A recent re-examination of this view has led to its complete modification.*

The *Bos* of the European Quaternary period consisted in fact of one species only, the numerous types described being merely variations of it. The *Bos longifrons*, which is also called *Bos brachyceros*, did not appear until the Post-glacial period; a small species of ox has never been found in the Quaternary sites of Europe, and the multiplication of the species occurred at a much later date as a result of domestication. The error made in classifying the oxen on the walls of Palaeolithic caves as two distinct species is due to the fact that the sexual dimorphism of *Bos primigenius* was very pronounced: this is evident from a comparison of a male with a female skull – the difference in size is enormous. In the case of the domestic ox, this dimorphism is still very considerable. There is every reason to accept this explanation for the oxen at Lascaux, since

* F. Koby, 'Y a-t-il eu à Lascaux un Bos longifrons?', *Bull. de la Soc. Préhist. française*, Vol. LI, fasc. 9–10, Nov. 1954, pp. 434–41.

the massive type shows the attributes of a bull and the slightly built type does not.

The Ox represented at Lascaux in fact is none other than the Aurochs of the ancient writers, the *Urus* that Caesar encountered 2,000 years ago in the Hercynian forests.* For a long time the aurochs was hunted by the Gauls as choice game, and its numbers had already decreased by the beginning of the Christian era. In the reign of Clovis (A.D. 488) it was so rare that no one but the king had the right to hunt it. Its last places of refuge in France were in the Pyrenees and the Vosges, from whence it disappeared about the twelfth century. Some herds continued to exist in the remoter regions of Europe, however. Gesner † records that in the sixteenth century the aurochs had disappeared from the Black Forest but was still to be found in the wild forests around Warsaw. The last forest where it was known to survive was near Sochaczew, about 50 miles from Warsaw; it is even known that the last representative of the species was an old female specimen which died in 1627.

There is also reason to believe that at that period the race had not been pure for a considerable time and had been crossed with animals which had escaped from domestication. Today, the wild cattle of Camargue is the species which most closely resembles the Quaternary aurochs, although they are smaller in size and of lighter build. In the Berlin Zoological Garden an attempt was made before the war to reproduce the primitive type by crossing specimens of various races showing characteristics closely resembling those of the aurochs. The experiment was begun in 1931 and, after fifteen years of selection, the Director, Dr L. Heck, believed that he had succeeded in breeding a perfectly stable race showing all the known characteristics of the primitive aurochs.

Both ancient treatises on hunting and the early naturalists provide a certain amount of information on the appearance

---

* *Les Mammifères sauvages d'Europe*, pp. 197–205.
† Swiss naturalist, 1516–65.

and habits of the aurochs. It was of enormous size: apparently the fossil aurochs was about 6 ft 6 in. to the withers, and its horns were sometimes more than 3 ft long.* In spite of the fact that ancient writers agree in describing it as a very large animal (slightly smaller than the elephant, Caesar wrote), the aurochs of historic times was smaller in size than the fossil aurochs, but taller and more powerful than the domesticated animal. The males were brown-black or black, the cows and the calves lighter in colour – red-brown with a white dorsal line.† The horns were long and whitish with black tips, the hair of the coat was longer than that of the domesticated animal, and the hair on the forehead curly.

These details correspond closely to the animals painted on the walls at Lascaux. The kind of tuft shown between the horns (Plates 7 and 9), which is also to be found on similar paintings in other caves, probably represents the curly hair on the forehead. The variety of the horns, which is such a striking feature of prehistoric paintings, may well have been a characteristic of the living animals of the period, for the horns of the domesticated animal of today vary enormously. At Lascaux the horns of the cows are more curved than those of the black bulls.

The forest was the home of the aurochs of historic times. It was an extremely strong animal, agile, fierce, and difficult to approach, and it fed on acorns, leaves, and shoots, etc. It is thought by some authorities that its favoured habitat was thin forests and glades, its natural surroundings thickets interspersed with grassland (Heck), and that it fed mainly on grass. The Camargue cattle, which live in a semi-wild state, move in herds led by an old cow, not by a bull, and in regions of extensive cattle-breeding – for example, the pampas of South

* Boule et Piveteau, *Les Fossiles*, p. 727.

† This difference between the coats of the male and the female at Lascaux is of importance for the chronological study of the paintings there. The black males and the red females do not necessarily correspond to different periods and styles.

America – the cattle live in complete freedom and likewise move in herds of about thirty to fifty in number. Like the horse of late Palaeolithic times, the aurochs was probably adapted to a temperate or cold, but not glacial, climate.

BISON

At Lascaux, bison are relatively few and they vary considerably in style. The only example in the painted chambers,* and according to Breuil the oldest painting in the cave, is painted in wide red bands and few details are shown (Plate 16). The bison of the scene in the Shaft (Plate 35) may also belong to an early period, but it shows characteristics of technique and style so unusual that it is almost impossible to place it chronologically. In the Main Gallery a painted and engraved bison is shown in association with a group of horses, likewise painted and engraved, with which it is contemporaneous (Fig. 16). The two bison shown back to back in the same Gallery (Plate 41) are male animals. They are represented with bristling manes and curious long horns standing well out from the mass of hair. Since one horn only is shown, and, in contrast with all the other animals of the cave, the technique of 'twisted perspective' has clearly not been used, Breuil regards them as the only Magdalenian figures at Lascaux. An engraved bison whose tail seems to lash the walls of the Chamber of Felines is probably of the same age as the engravings as a whole. There is also at least one very fine engraved head of a bison in the Lateral Passage.

Bison remains are very plentiful in the archaeological levels of the Upper Palaeolithic; at the end of the Magdalenian they become rarer. It must be noted, however, that, owing to the difficulty of distinguishing the remains of the *Bos* from those of the bison, writers, when studying the fauna of various sites,

* Abbé Breuil also reported a purplish bison in the Hall of the Bulls, but the writer could not find it.

sometimes merely mention the presence of a large 'bovid' without giving any details.

At an advanced phase of Magdalenian art there is a noticeable increase in the number of bison represented in caves. The great majority of the polychromes of Altamira and Font-de-Gaume are bison, but in the earlier periods of the evolution of cave art they are often portrayed with other species. They are present at Altamira and Font-de-Gaume in the phases prior to the polychromes, and they are numerous at Les Combarelles, Les Trois Frères, Niaux, Pech-Merle, Le Portel, and La Mouthe, etc.

Unlike the figures of equids or large oxen, the bison at Lascaux are not represented with peculiar characteristics distinguishing them from the bison of other Palaeolithic caves. Horns and heads embedded in thick fleece, enormous dorsal humps, and tails often erect in an attitude of rage are the most noteworthy characteristics at Lascaux as elsewhere. Three bison in the Main Gallery are represented with horns standing well out from the fleece, but this may be due to lack of skill on the part of the artist. In the middle of one of the two bison shown back to back, there is a large red irregular mark. Every spring the bison sheds its coat and large bare reddish patches are left on its body for a period which may last for as long as two or three months; so this red mark on the Lascaux bison may be an attempt to represent one of these seasonal bare places on the body of the animal.

At the present time there are still two species of bison surviving – the European bison (*Bison bonasus*) and the American bison. The Quaternary bison (*Bison priscus*) bore a closer resemblance to the latter.

The European bison * is a smaller forest variety of the Quaternary bison. The Quaternary bison inhabited the steppes and disappeared towards the end of the glacial period, when the forest began to encroach upon the immense tracts of steppe-

* *Les Mammifères sauvages d'Europe*, pp. 109–97.

land; the European bison has survived in Europe up to the present. There was a time when bison were hunted by Germanic peoples, and they had almost disappeared in Gaul under the Merovingians. They were reported in Prussia in the eighteenth century, however, and even later in the Caucasus and the forest of Bielowitza, where there were still 737 wild bison in 1914. During World War I they were all killed, but the herd was restarted later from animals of pure stock either privately owned or in zoological gardens. In 1949 the total world figure was 110 beasts, most of them crossed with some Caucasian stock, which is now completely extinct. Bison are extremely powerful animals. There is an account of one specimen killed in Prussia in 1555 which was more than 12 ft long and 6 ft high. Even allowing for a certain amount of exaggeration, these animals were undoubtedly gigantic creatures, comparable in size to the beasts hunted by Palaeolithic man.

The American bison is larger than the European species, but its general outline is similar. It has the enormous dorsal hump, and a mass of hair forming a beard under its chin, but its fleece is thicker. It was still very common at the beginning of the nineteenth century – it is said that there were 'hundreds of thousands' – when it lived in the vast plains in the middle and west of the United States and Canada. The Indians hunted it for food and used its skin to make garments and tepees when the species was in its heyday, and its disappearance cannot be attributed to them or to a change in climatic conditions. Its massacre began with the first pioneers; and when the prairies were transformed into immense fields of corn and some protection against the terrible destruction wrought by herds of bison had to be found, its extermination continued. In 1900 only a few herds remained in the remote valleys of Montana and Nevada, and it was about that date when Reserves were created in the United States and Canada. In 1920 a last herd of wild bison which had fled to refuge in the north was found in the region of the Great Slave River, about 400 miles from the

Arctic Circle. The territory was immediately proclaimed a National Park, and the species is now well protected and shows no sign of becoming extinct.

The bison is an animal of temperate or cold countries. The European variety is a forest animal with a liking for humid or even marshy ground, whereas the American bison is an animal of the steppes; its natural habitat is the great prairie, and it would seem to have fled to the forests of the far north merely to seek refuge. Both species are gregarious and live in herds, except the old males which live alone and only join the herd at the rutting season in the month of August. This is the period of the great battles between the males which end in the death, or more often the flight, of the weaker animal.

THE CERVIDAE

The *cervidae* occupy a relatively important place among the fauna of Lascaux. They are represented in paintings and engravings of both early and late dates, but most of the figures were executed towards the end of the period of the cave's decoration. Among the best figures the most outstanding are those of the frieze of swimming deer (Plates 33 and 42), which are superposed on the head and shoulders of a horse of the fluffy mane series, and the deer of the Chamber of Engravings, the earliest of which are painted and engraved, and the latest engraved only (Plate 22) and superposed on the large bovids of the series of animals in flat black wash.

It is noteworthy that the cervids of Lascaux are homogeneous in type. The perspective of the antlers and the hoofs and the placing of the ear scarcely vary from one period to another, though the pattern of the antlers may be divided into a few types which possibly correspond to particular stages of artistic evolution. Two examples (Fig. 22*g* and *h*) are very strange with the tines grouped in pairs along the entire length of the central beam. They are probably contemporaneous and belong to a fairly early phase. A third example of the same date also shows an extraordinary arrangement of the branches (Fig. 22g). A very small animal, also of early date, since it is overlaid by a large bull painted in black bands, carries a palm with numerous tines, which gives it the appearance of a fallow deer (Fig. 22b). In the Main Gallery the branches of the antlers are more uniform and often show three main tines. One figure has large antlers which are undoubtedly more flattened than the others, but this is an exceptional case (Fig. 22a).

The deer at Lascaux have never been studied from a palae-ontological point of view, but it is probable that all the animals represented there are the species *Cervus elaphus*, the deer which frequents our European forests, with the possible addition of a few fallow deer.

The average length of the existing deer of European forests * is about 6 ft, though some have been known to measure nearly 9 ft, and the average animal weighs about 330–440 lb. The colour of its coat varies: it is red or yellowish in summer and darkens in winter. The hind is much smaller and of lighter colour. One fact is worthy of particular mention – all the cervids at Lascaux are stags with magnificent antlers: no hinds are depicted. It is a well-known fact, of course, that only stags bear antlers, which are usually shed in March, grow again almost immediately, and reach their full development about June. From this fact it may be concluded that the deer of Lascaux were portrayed in the period between June of one year and March of the next. For either aesthetic, religious, or utilitarian reasons, the artists appear to have been greatly attracted by these antlers.

The deer is essentially a forest animal, but it will readily leave the forests to graze in the plains and feed in the thickets; because of its agility it is also as much at home in the mountains as in the lowlands. It swims with ease and crosses arms of

* *Op. cit.*, pp. 128–39. Illustrations of antlers very similar to those of Lascaux are to be found in H. Kreig, 'Das Hirschgeweih, eine vierte Vorlesung', *Die Naturwissenschaften*, 33rd year, 15 July 1946, Vol. 6, pp. 175–82.

the sea as well as rivers. It lives in herds usually consisting of one old stag, hinds, and their young; but it would appear that outside the rutting season the herds are not very stable and the stags frequently leave them. In fine weather the stags live separately or in small herds, and the frieze of swimming deer may very likely depict one of these fluctuating summer groups. About September the rutting season begins, and continues into October. The great battles take place then, and perhaps one of these may be depicted in an engraving in the Chamber of Engravings, though, if this is so, the movement would seem to be rather inadequately portrayed. Deer live on plants, leaves, various fruits, and the bark of trees; their habitat is the temperate forestlands of Europe and they are never found in the extreme southerly zones (there is none in Italy), or further north than the centre of Scandinavia.

THE IBEX

Like the ox-tribe and the cervids, ibexes are relatively numerous at Lascaux. Two are painted, seven painted and engraved (Plates 26 and 27), and the remaining figures are mainly small engraved silhouettes in the Lateral Passage and the Chamber of Engravings. Their total number is probably about fifteen, whereas there are only five at Font-de-Gaume, all dating from the first period of the cave's decoration, and nine at Les Combarelles. At Le Portel there is only one, and there is one at Pech-Merle also. At Altamira, on the contrary, ibexes, together with deer and horses, are predominant in the early paintings.

Whether painted or engraved, the ibexes at Lascaux are generally somewhat stylized. The body is incomplete (except in the case of one of the painted ibex): only the line of the chest is represented, the line of the back being left unfinished. The horns are long and thrown right back and, curiously enough, the transverse knots, so clear on the present-day ibex and on certain prehistoric portrayals, are not shown. The series of dots forming the outline of some of the horns (Plate 26) may be intended to show these knots, but, as other figures in the cave are similarly outlined, this interpretation seems unlikely.

The ibex (*Capra ibex*) * is not extinct in Europe. At one time this species was abundant in the Alps, but in the nineteenth century it was on the point of extinction. Vigorous protective measures, however, enabled several herds to be restarted, and there are now six in Switzerland totalling 1,000 head, and others in the Bavarian Alps.

The male ibex is a powerful beast measuring from 3 to 4 ft from the root of the tail to the chest, and some specimens weigh about 220 lb. The old males turn dark in colour, sometimes almost black, but in spring their coat lightens to a chocolate shade and the line of the neck and back becomes almost white. Their legs are short, their skulls broad, and their ears small. The horns of the male are very long – they measure at least 2 ft and sometimes even 3 ft – and slightly curved. When throwing their heads backwards, some males nearly touch their tails with the tips of their horns. The transverse knots are clearly visible on the frontal curve. The female is very different from the male. It is much smaller, its horns are more like those of a goat, its coat is lighter in colour – a rather pinkish fawn – its head is grey, and its belly white. On the strength of these differences, above all the dissimilarity of the horns, the ibexes at Lascaux can be identified as males. One small engraved figure in the frieze of seven ibexes in the Main Gallery could be a female, but a similar interpretation of the head and shoulders painted in red above the bistre ibex in the Painted Gallery is less acceptable.

It is not clearly established that the natural habitat of the ibex is in the mountain, for it has been found in nearly every Upper Palaeolithic site. It may be that it is found in precipitous and remote places today because only here could it find a

* *Op. cit.*, p. 155–68.

safe refuge from hunters. The ibex is not a forest animal; though it may sometimes descend to less mountainous regions, it avoids dense forests and seeks out glades and thinly wooded areas. It can bear severe cold, but it invariably makes for sunny slopes. It feeds on all kinds of plants. The males live in small herds sometimes totalling about thirty animals; the females live with their young. The rutting season begins in December and scarcely ever leads to combat between the bucks; the two ibexes confronting each other at Lascaux are most probably depicted at the customary evening play of this animal.

THE MUSK-OX AND THE REINDEER

On the walls of the Chamber of Engravings, superposed on other images, the figures of a reindeer and a musk-ox (*ovibos*)* have been discovered. Both portrayals are very poor. The musk-ox is thought to be recognizable by its two wide-spreading horns with a marked forward curve, but it has not yet been conclusively identified. No reproduction of this figure has ever been published.

If we accept this identification, it provides an important indication of the evolution of the fauna at the time of the cave's use. Reindeer and musk-ox are circumpolar species associated with a tundra vegetation. The reindeer (*Rangifer tarandus*) is still common in the north of Eurasia and in North America; the musk-ox (*Ovibos moschatus*) is extinct in Europe, though there are still a few herds surviving in Greenland and in the north of Canada. The superposition of these two engravings on others which are undoubtedly among the latest in the cave would seem to indicate that the last use of Lascaux corresponded to a change-over to a distinctly colder climate with a concomitant change in the fauna.

---

* The musk-ox was discovered fairly recently by Abbé Glory.

THE FELINES

All the felines at Lascaux (about six or seven in all) are grouped together in the Chamber of Felines (Plate 34 and Fig. 18), though there is possibly another with open and menacing jaws engraved on the walls of the Chamber of Engravings. None of these figures is painted. Although the style is somewhat rudimentary, they are easily identified by their broad round heads, upright ears, long tails, and powerful paws.

There are not a great many representations of felines in cave art, but there are some examples in almost every cave, including Font-de-Gaume, Les Combarelles, Les Trois Frères, and Le Combel (one of the galleries of Pech-Merle). Like those at Lascaux, most of the figures in these caves are engraved: the only painted feline known is at Le Combel. In the caves in which they appear felines invariably are associated with horses.

The animal thus portrayed in practically every cave is undoubtedly the terrible cave lion (*Felis leo*), which lived in Europe, including Great Britain, and in Africa during the whole of the Pleistocene. It disappeared from our regions only at the end of the Glacial epoch or the very beginning of the post-glacial period. It is never found in Neolithic sites. In a smaller form it survived until historic times in the south-east of Europe and in Asia Minor.* At the present time it exists only in India in a Reserve, and in Africa, where a few specimens still live in a completely wild state, although the majority are also protected in a Reserve.

The lion is a comparatively gregarious animal: it is not unusual to see a pride of from ten to twenty animals. Although it once lived in much colder regions, its habitat today is limited to hot countries, and of all the animals at Lascaux it is the species best adapted to a really warm climate. The outlines of the felines in the Chamber of Felines are so rudimentary that it is impossible to determine whether the figures are male or

* Boule et Piveteau, *Les Fossiles*, p. 792.

female. Manes are not represented, which might imply that the animals depicted are females, but this omission is very common in prehistoric art. When manes are represented, they are comparatively insignificant, though a lion at Les Combarelles has quite a fine one. It may be that in the Quaternary period lions did not have such magnificent manes as they have today.

THE BEAR

At the time of Lascaux's use the cave bear had already been extinct for a long time, and the small bear painted in the Hall of the Bulls is undoubtedly a brown bear (*Ursus arctos*). Like felines, these animals are not common in cave art, but a great number of caves contain at least one figure. There are several at Les Trois Frères, one at Pech-Merle, one at Font-de-Gaume in the earliest series, and nineteen at Les Combarelles, but this last figure is quite exceptional. Like lions, bears are almost invariably engraved. There is another painted bear, however, in the cave of Aldène.

The brown bear of Europe still survives in Scandinavia, in the Pyrenees, and in the mountains of Eastern Europe. It adapts itself to severe cold in winter by hibernating in rocks or in the hollows of trees. It is a harmless carnivorous animal, its main foods being berries, fruits, small mammals, and sometimes fish.

THE RHINOCEROS

The Rhinoceros (Plate 43) in the Shaft of the Dead Man is one of the most impressive animals at Lascaux, for, though it is common knowledge that there were once wild horses, wild oxen, ibexes, deer, and even bison, bears, and mammoths in the peaceful regions of Western France, it is generally forgotten that the rhinoceros was a typical member of the cold fauna of the Quaternary era.

The earliest type of Quaternary rhinoceros was the *Rhino-*

ceros merckii. The *Rhinoceros tichorhinus,* with partitioned nostrils, was a later type, better adapted to the cold because of its thick woolly fleece. It is generally supposed that the rhinoceros represented by Palaeolithic artists is the *Rhinoceros tichorhinus,* but Professor Zeuner recently put forward the suggestion that the rhinoceros at Lascaux is a *Rhinoceros merckii.* This question has not yet been settled conclusively.

The rhinoceros is a rare figure in decorated caves; possibly it was almost extinct at the peak period of Quaternary art. In addition to the rhinoceros of the Shaft, there is a rather poor engraving of another(?) on the vault of the Chamber of Felines. The head of yet another has been reported in the lower part of the belly of one of the bulls of the Great Hall, but to the writer this seems unlikely. There are two figures of rhinoceroses at Font-de-Gaume, two at Les Combarelles: one(?) at Les Trois Frères, two at La Mouthe, one on a rock slab at La Ferassie, one at Casares, and one at La Pileta. In the latest paintings and engravings not a single example is depicted: none exists among the polychromes of Font-de-Gaume or Altamira, or in the engravings of Magdalenian V at Teyjat. The frieze of three rhinoceroses in the recently discovered cave of Rouffignac is quite exceptional.

In Europe the rhinoceros is completely extinct, but one species still survives in Asia and another in Africa. Unlike the rhinceros of the Quaternary hunters, the rhinceros of Asia, except for a single species in Sumatra, has one horn only, and its skin is thrown into deep folds forming a hard shell. The African rhinoceros, which has two horns and no folds on its skin, is closer in appearance to the rhinoceros of the Quaternary. The frontal horn is always longer than the other; in the female it is over 3 ft long and has been known to measure 4–5 ft; in the male it is somewhat smaller.

The rhinoceros is a herbivorous animal and feeds on grasses and plants. Like the lion, the present-day species exists only in hot or very hot regions, whereas the Quaternary species, like the mammoth, was one of the most characteristic animals of the cold fauna and was extremely well adapted to the cold. Woolly-coated rhinoceroses survived for a long time in Siberia, and specimens are discovered periodically in late alluvial deposits of this region. Some have been found almost intact where they had lain frozen for thousands of years. If a map showing discoveries of rhinoceroses in Siberia since the eighteenth century up to 1910 is compared with another showing discoveries of mammoths in that area over the same period, it will be seen that the area of distribution of the rhinoceros was possibly somewhat less northerly than that of the mammoth.*

Some fossil aurochs have also been found in the same regions and in similar circumstances. The mammoths were found in the extreme north, in the peninsulas of Taimyr and Ghydansk, at the mouth of the Lena, and as far distant as the isles of Liakhov and New Siberia, whereas the most northerly discovery of a rhinoceros was made at Verkhoyansk in 1910. The majority of the other discoveries were made in regions much farther to the south.

The Lascaux artists depicted other subjects besides these animals – a bird, a man, an imaginary animal, possibly one or two plants, and innumerable signs, some of which are recognizable as weapons such as darts or harpoons. The study of these subjects, however, properly belongs to an examination of the meaning and purpose of the paintings.

CLIMATIC OSCILLATIONS OF THE END OF THE LAST GLACIAL PERIOD

In conclusion, it can be said that the Lascaux fauna provides some reasonably accurate indications of the contemporary climate and geographic environment (vegetation and animal associations). The majority of the animals represented are asso-

* E. W. Pfizenmayer, Les Mammouths de Sibérie, 1939, map, pp. 8–9.

ciated with a temperate, but rather cold, climate; the only exceptions are the rhinoceros, the musk-ox, and the reindeer. The
last two animals are among the latest representations in the
cave and may perhaps coincide with the onset of a distinctly
colder climate at the end of the period of the cave's use; on
the other hand it is not certain that these figures have been cor-
rectly identified. It is not inconceivable that the rhinoceros
may have adapted itself to a temperate climate more easily
than the mammoth, for example, and the absence of mammoth and reindeer is likewise an indication that the period of
the highest artistic achievement at Lascaux did not correspond
to a cold oscillation of the last glaciation.

Apart from the possible musk-ox and reindeer, it would be
idle to try to classify the figures represented at Lascaux into
climatic periods: horses and bovids are represented in every
period, whereas deer and bison are possibly commoner in the
second period of the cave's use.

The foregoing data are of little statistical value, however,
for they are applicable to too few instances; and it is not
known whether this change in the proportionate numbers of
the various animals depicted corresponded to a climatic
change (moderate temperature, pluvial, etc.), to a change of
environment (relative increase of forest over steppe or vice
versa), or to new interests on the part of the artists. It would be
useful to have statistical tables for Palaeolithic caves as a whole,
for no conclusions can be drawn from the study of one cave
alone.

Animals of the steppe such as the horse or the bison, and
specifically forest animals like deer, undoubtedly lived side by
side at the time of the frequentation of Lascaux. As deer appear to be more numerous in the later artistic series, is it to
be concluded that this indicates the encroachment of forest
on steppe? Perhaps too much importance should not be attached to what may well have been merely a change in the
artists' choice of subject in no way connected with the actual

TABLE 3

**TYPICAL HABITAT AND CLIMATIC CONDITIONS OF THE
MOST IMPORTANT ANIMALS AT LASCAUX**

Species	Habitat	Climate	Remarks
Equus caballus	Steppes or forests	Cold or temperate	
Bos primigenius	Steppes or forests	Cold or temperate	
Bison priscus	Steppes or forests	Cold or temperate	If the red patch on one of the bison represents a shedding of the coat, the animal has been depicted in the spring. If Plate 41 depicts the end of a combat between males, the animals have been portrayed in the rutting season, about the month of August
Cervus elaphus	Woods or forests (but not steppes)	Considerably more temperate than the above-mentioned	The large size of the antlers indicates that the animals were portrayed between the months of June and March. The battles between males take place between September and October
Capra ibex	Steppes or wooded areas (but not forest)	Cold or temperate	
Felis leo	Steppes or wooded areas	Temperate or warm	
Ursus arctos	Forests	Cold or temperate	
Rhinoceros	Forests	Cold	

numbers of the game living on their hunting grounds. In the absence of other concrete facts, it is more prudent to conclude that at that time the valley of the Vézère probably consisted of steppeland interspersed with thin forests. The average temperature could only have been a few degrees – probably two or three – lower than today's temperature.*

From the evidence of the charcoals found at Lascaux, conifers were plentiful – possibly predominant. Unfortunately, laboratory tests have not revealed from what vegetable fibres the rope found in the Chamber of Felines was made.

These data on the fauna appear to certain writers to be contradictory to the archaeological dating of Lascaux, which assigns the works to about the end of the Perigordian, and to the dating by C14, which places the age of the cave at about 15,000 years. If the fauna and flora of the end of the Perigordian had already lost their glacial characteristics at this latter period (13,000 B.C.), the interval of time before the Post-Glacial period would appear to be insufficient to allow for the appearance and stabilization of a new indisputably cold fauna and flora corresponding to Magdalenian cultures, for whose evolution a much longer period of time is generally thought to be necessary. This problem is undoubtedly a difficult one to solve, but, thanks to new geological data, it can now be approached with more confidence.

The climatic oscillations in Europe over the Pleistocene in general and each glacial period in particular are much more complex than was believed fifty years ago. They are not definitely established, and little is known of the corresponding climatic fluctuations throughout the rest of the world; but it has been confirmed with certainty that at the end of the fourth glaciation both Europe and North America were affected by

---

* According to various calculations, at the peak of the fourth glaciation the average temperature was only 5° C. (7° maximum) lower than the present temperature. Cf. Flint, *Glacial Geology and the Pleistocene Epoch*, New York, 1949, pp. 455–6.

climatic oscillations of comparatively short duration in terms of geology. The problem of determining into which of these periods of oscillation Lascaux should be placed has yet to be solved.

If one of the tables showing the climatic variations affecting North-western Europe over the last 20,000 years is studied as an example, it will be seen that within this space of time there were two cold periods, one of which might include the cold period of the end of the Magdalenian. The date of the later cold period lies between 10,000 and 9000 B.C.; the earlier one ended at approximately 15,000 B.C., i.e. 17,000 years ago. These data were established for North-western Europe on the basis of a study of peat pollens. Western France has not been studied in the same detail, but there was an undoubted similarity in the climatic variations of the two regions, although the valley of the Vézère and all the region of Périgord were clearly always slightly warmer.

It is noteworthy that the data obtained from a test of the charcoal from Lascaux (13,000 B.C. approximately) can readily be embodied in the above table drawn up on a completely different basis. The pentultimate temperate oscillation (the one in which we are now living being the last) of the last glaciation lasted about 5,000 years – from 14,500 to 10,000 B.C.* In other words, it began about 16,500 years ago and ended some 12,000 years ago.

During this period, which was less cold than the preceding and the following periods, the tundra in the north was replaced by a vegetation of pine and birch. Further south, where possibly pine and birch had never ceased to exist, the change was doubtless marked by an increase of vegetation. At first sight, the placing of Lascaux in that period would seem to be indicated.

* These figures are quoted only to give a general idea of dates; there was an imperceptible and probably long transition between one climatic period and the next.

TABLE 4

CHANGES OF CLIMATE AND VEGETATION IN N.-W. EUROPE

After Flint and Morris (Flint, *Glacial Geology*, p. 490)

	Climatic Changes	Vegetation
A.D. 1955 0	Sub-Atlantic (Cool and damp)	Increase of beech
B.C. 2000	Sub-boreal (Warm and dry)	Diminution of mixed forest Increase of pine
4000	Atlantic (Warm and damp)	Appearance of beech and hornbeam Prevalence of mixed forest (oak, elm, and lime)
6000	Boreal (Warm and dry)	Prevalence of hazel Diminution of pine
8000	Preboreal (Cold)	Prevalence of pine Birch and Pine
10,000	Arctic (Cold)	Tundra
12,000 14,000	Sub-Arctic (Less cold)	Birch and Pine
16,000 18,000 20,000	Arctic (Cold) Würm III	Tundra

The relatively temperate oscillation was followed by a recurrence of the cold, and the forest again receded. The date of this cold wave was about 10,000 B.C., and it was of short duration – about 1,000 years. The whole of the Magdalenian era could hardly fall within this short period, but the evolution of the Magdalenian cultures could well have begun in the preceding period of sub-arctic climate.

CHAPTER 4

THE PROBLEMS OF THE INTERPRETATION OF CAVE ART

The Classic Theories

THROUGHOUT the whole of the nineteenth century little was known of Prehistoric art apart from a few examples of decorated *art mobilier* and small sculptured or engraved fragments which were considered to be mere manifestations of a considerably developed artistic aptitude. When the first discoveries of painted or engraved figures on rock surfaces were made they did not arouse any particular speculation as to their significance, for it had yet to be proved that these paintings and engravings at Altamira, Chabot, Pair-non-Pair, La Mouthe, then at Les Combarelles and Font-de-Gaume, did in fact date from Palaeolithic times. In their early reports, Daleau, Rivière, then Capitan, Breuil, and Peyrony naturally concentrated solely on the authenticity of the works and their contemporaneity with Quaternary fauna.

At the end of the nineteenth and the beginning of the twentieth centuries, however, a very important stage in the study of primitive cultures was reached. There was no more talk of wild and backward 'savages': the term 'primitive peoples' was now used and efforts were made to find some clue to their way of life and mental outlook. Frazer was born in 1854, Dürkheim in 1858, and Lévy-Brühl in 1857; Frazer's *Golden Bough*, which aroused enormous interest, was published in 1890, and *Les Formes élémentaires de la vie religieuse* by Dürkheim in 1912. This was the period of the great controversies on animism, fetishism, and totemism; and there was much discussion whether, as Spencer and Taylor believed, the cult of the souls of ancestors was primordial, or preceded by a cult of the forces of nature as Müller maintained. The theory of totemism, originated by Frazer and supported by Dürkheim, was much in vogue, and so too was the theory of magic. These ideas gradually spread among the general public and also invaded the fields of other sciences, such as prehistory. Spencer and Gillen brought back from Australia a comprehensive report of primitive communities plying industries similar to those of Palaeolithic Man and whose art, in certain of its aspects, was reminiscent of cave art. The notion that when he was not hunting Palaeolithic Man spent his leisure haphazardly decorating any bone fragments or pieces of stone which happened to be at hand was now dismissed with ridicule.

In 1903 the first detailed study of the interpretation of Palaeolithic figures based on the theory of magic was published in *L'Anthropologie*.* The author, Salomon Reinach, who was at that time curator of the Musée des Antiquités Nationales at Saint-German-en-Laye, basing his argument on information obtained from the study of Australian aboriginal communities, suggested that the purpose of Palaeolithic art, which portrayed almost exclusively the animals of the period, was to put a spell on the hunted game in order to attract large numbers to the vicinity of the caves. His theory, though still somewhat elementary, since the main argument in favour of the belief in the magic purpose of Palaeolithic art – the representation of darts and wounds – was not even mentioned, enjoyed considerable success, and it did, in fact, contain the germ of the more comprehensive explanations which were put forward in the following decades as and when discoveries were made. Above all, it marked a new approach to the problem on the part of all the investigators of the twentieth century. From that time onwards prehistoric art was regarded as the material evidence of beliefs and rituals similar to those still held and practised by primitive communities today, and all attempts at its interpretation were based on comparative ethno-

* *Salomon Reinach, 'L'Art et la Magie', L'Anthropologie, 1903, pp. 125–36.*

graphy. Broadly speaking, these attempts can be divided into two categories – one stressing the theory of hunting or sympathetic magic, the other, of less importance, the theories of totemism, primitive religion, belief in a spirit world, etc. It was generally agreed, however, that there was a certain degree of artistic impulse in the creation of Palaeolithic art, but the theory of art for art's sake was completely abandoned.

The conviction that Palaeolithic art is linked to a still unknown system of rites and beliefs is based on the fact that the art of all primitive societies is founded on magic or religious belief. Comparative ethnography acknowledges that a universal phenomenon is likely to be of very ancient origin; therefore it seems legitimate to suppose that Palaeolithic art was likewise based on religious or magical beliefs.

Such an explanation of cave art is readily acceptable. Could a cave like Lascaux have been anything but a sanctuary? It was undoubtedly never an occupation site, or a place of frequent assembly; for, if it had been used as either one or the other, cooking refuse and other débris would have been found, and objects lost and forgotten by successive generations discovered in the archaeological layers. Moreover, it is clear to anyone who has worked in the depths of these caves that it is impossible to remain there for a long period at a stretch: they are cold, damp, the darkness is impenetrable, and, so soon as a fire is lit, smoke accumulates in the chambers and the atmosphere becomes unbearable.

Many of the paintings at Lascaux undoubtedly convey the impression of decorative intention, and it seems quite clear that they were created with some degree of aesthetic consciousness. But it is difficult thus to explain the engravings in the Chamber of Felines, for example, high up on the walls of a narrow, steep tunnel and visible only from a most uncomfortable position; or the medley of figures in the Chamber of Engravings, which are so difficult to decipher; or the numerous engravings on the small dome overlooking the mouth of the

Shaft of the Dead Man. None of these figures is easy to locate and they were certainly not intended for the mere adornment of the cave.

In other caves this absence of a purely decorative motive is even more striking. At Niaux, the first paintings start more than 800 yards from the entrance; at Le Combel, three fantastic animals (Plate 44) with rhinoceroses' bodies and antelopes' heads are painted in a small chamber whose only entrance is a narrow, angled opening quite inaccessible to all but the slim; and at Arcy-sur-Cure the engravings are discovered only after a painful crawl of about 80 yards over slippery clay and sharp-pointed calcite. Such remote recesses, difficult of access and laborious of approach, are almost as numerous as the painted and engraved caves themselves. The placing of all these figures in remote parts of dark caverns seems to bear witness to a pursuit of the arduous, the magical, and the sacred.

We are still far from understanding the purpose and meaning of these underground sanctuaries. The richness and variety of Palaeolithic works of art may well indicate beliefs and rituals already complex. Various hypotheses have been put forward which are not wholly incompatible, and on one at least there is general agreement: some of the figures in cave art (all according to some authorities) were created with the aim of ensnaring game by magical forces, and thus ensuring the success of the hunt. Sympathetic magic is indeed a universally known practice which still survives in certain social strata of even the most advanced civilizations. In cave art there are numerous indications that Palaeolithic hunters tried to produce a material effect on a living creature by subjecting its image to whatever they desired the creature itself to experience.

At Lascaux and elsewhere, the subjects of cave paintings and engravings are almost invariably game such as horses, oxen, deer, and bison – precisely those animals representing the staple food of the time which therefore had to be hunted and killed. When other animals such as felines are portrayed, the circumstances are often different from those of the majority of the figures. The representation of various weapons piercing the animals or flying round about them provides the most convincing proof that the decoration of the caves was inspired by the motive of hunting magic. At Lascaux darts are painted and engraved across the bodies of various animals or around them; some of them are feathered, and the sharp point is often indicated by one or two small transverse strokes. A few harpoons are engraved on the walls of the Chamber of Engravings, and it is very likely that other weapons are also represented, but they have not yet been identified. Similar representations of various weapons are found in a great many caves.

Strokes radiating from the nostrils of an animal are usually interpreted as blood flowing from a wound, and patches or lines on its flank as the wound itself; they might equally well, however, be interpreted as the breath of life, or as a sign of rage. A cluster of such lines is seen projecting from the nostrils of one of the felines engraved at Lascaux. There is no unmistakable representation of a wound in the cave except for the wounded bison in the Shaft, though the large deer pierced by a dart in the Chamber of Engravings is undoubtedly the portrayal of an animal mortally wounded. Animals shown falling backwards and the various signs which could be interpreted as traps may well refer to prehistoric modes of trapping animals at which we can only guess. The theory of the ritual and magical significance of Palaeolithic art could apply to all these representations which are similar to those found in most caves.

The theory of sympathetic magic, however, does not explain all the representations in cave art, for the number of animals shown in association with darts and other weapons is very limited, and many more are shown in peaceful attitudes which in no way evoke either the hunt or sympathetic magic. In addition, certain figures raise specific problems. Some caves contain one or more human shapes depicted in a style completely different from that of the animals. Stiff and clumsy these figures are and barely recognizable as human beings. They are invariably small or of medium height, and their heads are particularly strange. Some have the head of a deer, a bison, a mammoth, or a bird, etc.; others, a sort of muzzle with very little human affinity. In addition to these semi-human representations, which completely belie the realism of cave art in general, many strange animals such as the monster of Lascaux (Plate 2), or imaginary combinations of various animals, or unknown creatures which could never have existed, are represented on the walls.

A magic significance is sometimes attributed to these semi-human figures also, and they are described as masked sorcerers practising unknown rites to ensure the success of the hunt; or as men wearing hunting-masks or disguises to enable them to approach their quarry without attracting its attention. These interpretations tally closely with the theory of sympathetic magic; animals masks are still used by hunters as far apart geographically as the Indians of North America and the Bushmen of South Africa – indeed, the custom of wearing such masks is widespread throughout the world.

Nevertheless, these explanations are unsatisfactory. Why should the sorcerer, who was probably also the artist of the tribe, portray his own image? A ritual ceremony is efficacious in itself, and there would appear to be no valid reason why it should be recorded on the rock surface. The walls and the stained glass of our churches evoke an image of the after-life and record the story of Christianity: they do not portray the ritual of the cult. The theory relating to hunting masks provides no explanation of the curious composite animals or of the schematic portrayals of the semi-human figures. If these representations depict beings wearing animal masks in order to deceive their quarry, surely the artists would have portrayed them with particular care and not drawn them in a few hasty strokes? It is clear that the answer to all the riddles is not to be found in the theory of hunting magic alone – other hypotheses must be examined, other explanations sought.

Numerous primitive religions still found in remote parts of the world share a fundamental belief in the kinship of members of the same group through common ancestry with one particular animal species, a plant, or even an object – the totem. The wide area over which belief in the totem is spread indicates its extremely ancient origin, and ever since the beginning of the twentieth century this belief has constantly been put forward as an explanation of Palaeolithic animal art.

Australian aboriginal communities provide the best examples of totemic societies. They are still very much alive and have often been the subject of research. The basic unit of such an Australian community is the clan, and each clan is characterized by a totem peculiar to it. A tribe is made up of a great many clans – several dozen, or even several hundreds – representing a great variety of totems. Indeed owing to the difficulty of finding a sufficiently large number of suitable animal or vegetable species, some totems are represented by a part only of an animal or plant.

The totem is sacred: the uninitiated are forbidden to look upon it and the place where it is enshrined in one form or another is regarded as a sanctuary. The killing of totem animals and the gathering of totem plants are prohibited. There are, of course, exceptions to this rule; a man might be forced to kill his totem animal in self-defence, for example, in which event purification rites would have to be performed. It is of great importance for the interpretation of prehistoric art to realize that the totem is essentially a symbol which can be represented in a variety of ways: by designs traced in the sand, by paintings or engravings on rock, by masks or tattooing, or even by bodily mutilation, and also by mime and dance. It can also be represented by lines or geometric designs comprehensible only to the initiated, as well as by more or less realistic representations.

It is easy to understand how these various aspects of the totem suggest a totemic interpretation of Palaeolithic art; but, at the same time, it is apparent that this interpretation is open to a great deal of criticism. Animal figures on the walls of caves may well represent sacred animals, and it is not unreasonable to suppose that they had a connexion with certain forms of the cult of totem-ancestors. These totem-ancestors, who were believed to be intermediaries between man and beast, may possibly be represented by the animal-headed beings present in almost every cave. This hypothesis was first put forward by Salomon Reinach at the end of the last century and supported later by Dr Hamy; it is mentioned by almost every writer on the meaning of prehistoric cave art – Breuil, Dechelette, and others – but none of them has ever set out to prove it.

In fact, critics of the theory have always been more numerous than its supporters; it can indeed be said to have been doomed almost from birth, for it immediately met with strong opposition, and few gave it unqualified support. It is scarcely possible to associate a Palaeolithic community and its art with totem beliefs known to be held by existing primitive communities. In a totemic community each clan has a particular totem of its own. If the structure of Palaeolithic communities had been based on totemism, Palaeolithic art would be characterized by a multiplicity of totemic symbols. Presumably each cave would normally have been used by one clan only and would therefore contain representations of one single species; or at least each period would be represented by one particular symbol. There would thus have been a cave of the Bison clan, for example, a cave of the Mammoth clan, etc. Palaeolithic caves undoubtedly show some concentration on the portrayal of particular species: the bovids at Lascaux, the bison at Font-de-Gaume, the horses at Les Combarelles are more numerous than other species, but many others are also depicted and vary little from one cave to another. This representation of several species of animal, several totems in one cave at one and the same period, is completely at variance with what is known of totemism as practised today. Moreover, portrayals of semi-human beings are never predominant in caves; and, if they represented totem-ancestors, some other explanation would have to be found for the animal processions accompanying them. For example, without being the ancestors of any particular clan, these animals could be associated with totemic myths concerning the origin and history of the group. This theory, which has never been fully explored, is less open to criticism than the suggestion that all the representations in a cave are to be interpreted as totems.

The variety of species represented in Palaeolithic art as a whole is limited to wild oxen, bison, equids – particularly horses, with a sprinkling of wild asses – cervids, reindeer, deer, ibexes, mammoths, rhinoceroses, carnivorous animals (lions, bears); fishes and birds are rare. This uniformity is in strange contrast with the multitude of totems seen in existing primitive communities. And if the signs depicted in caves were totemic symbols, some attempt would surely have been made to vary them from one cave to another, or from one clan or tribe to another; whereas, from the Dordogne to Spain the painted and engraved signs of Palaeolithic man show such a striking family resemblance that there has always been a tendency to interpret them collectively, some authorities describing them as 'huts', others as traps. The signs which cannot be included in these two categories show little variety: almost all of them are darts or punctuations.

Moreover, in existing primitive communities the totem is regarded as sacred, and the ban on killing or eating any totem animal or gathering any totem plant is universal; the presence of darts or wounds on the painted or engraved bodies of alleged totem animals is therefore sufficient to rule out the totem theory. A totem must be respected and venerated; it is taboo and an animal could not be both the totem-ancestor of a tribe and the hunters' customary quarry. Since the totemic interpretation is untenable and the theory of hunting and sympathetic magic inadequate to explain *all* the manifestations of prehistoric wall art, a multitude of the most diverse hypotheses has been put forward; some of them are plausible enough, but none of them provides any convincing proof. Indeed, their very diversity merely emphasizes the great complexity of the beliefs of Palaeolithic Man.

In their interpretation of Palaeolithic cave art, some of the hypotheses seek to cover the whole of Palaeolithic belief. The discovery of burials proves that, since the Mousterian era at least, that is to say well before the appearance of *Homo sapiens*, man believed in the supernatural, and quite probably certain forms of skull worship were practised. Although in Western Europe, at all events, there may have been a gap between the Mousterian and the early Perigordian cultures, this skull worship would appear to have been practised throughout the whole of the Upper Palaeolithic.* Finds of headless skeletons and isolated skulls or jaw-bones prove conclusively that the severance from the body of the bones of the face and skull was not fortuitous, but related to some custom of great antiquity based on a belief unknown to us. Certain of the burial practices indicate a fear of the corpse; it was sometimes bound, sometimes placed face downwards at the bottom of a ditch dug specially for its burial, and sometimes covered by large slabs of stone. These precautions are explainable only by a belief in the survival of the dead in one form or another.

On the strength of these facts various theories have been advanced concerning certain aspects of cave art. It has been suggested that the anthropoid figures represent spirits or ancestors. As long ago as 1918, Obermaier suggested that the geometrical signs could represent traps to ensnare hostile spirits

---

* Breuil and Lantier, *Les Hommes de la pierre ancienne*, pp. 289 ff.

who might prevent the success of the hunt. Such traps are still used in the Malay Peninsula. Breuil has often put forward the suggestion that these signs are not traps in the strict sense of the word, but rather 'resting-places' (*reposoirs*) where the spirits were believed to take refuge. Paul Wernert,* who has made a special study of Palaeolithic skull worship, has suggested that the anthropoid figures might be portrayals of ancestors; and several writers who do not subscribe to the theory of hunting masks or to the totemic theory in its entirety hold the belief that the semi-human, semi-animal figures are representations of mythical beings, perhaps dieties.

Palaeolithic human representations include a considerable number of sculptured and engraved female figures, whose sexual characteristics are emphasized. Apart from steatopygous figurines, which are distributed over an area far wider than that of cave art, such figures have been found in the cave of Pech-Merle (Lot), at Laussel (Dordogne) (Plate 39), at Angles-sur-Anglin (Vienne), and at Penne (Tarn). These female figures are usually considered within the framework of cave art as a whole, but the writer is of the opinion † that they are generally sited in particular circumstances and associated with different beliefs and rituals from those which inspired the animal representations in the depths of the caves. Pech-Merle is one of the rare sites which is at present known to us where female figures are depicted in an underground sanctuary.

These engraved figures at Pech-Merle are thought to be the oldest works of art in the cave. They have been traced with the fingers on the clay surface of the ceiling of the main chamber and consist of female silhouettes somewhat coarsely associated with mammoths. The breasts are the most prominent

* Paul Wernert, 'Le culte des crânes', *Histoire Générale des Religions*, Paris, 1948, pp. 53–97, Fig. 85.

† See Introduction, pp. 34–5 *et passim* and A. Laming, *La Signification de l'art pariétal paléolithique* (in the press).

characteristic and they have been depicted with care. The figures are considered by the discoverer to represent a series of female idols, mother-goddesses, connected in some way with a maternity cult.* In 1949 the gallery of Le Combel, which was probably part of the underground structure of Pech-Merle, was discovered, and in a small chamber accessible only through a narrow cleft a painting of a group of imaginary animals with massive bodies and slender heads found. The vaulted ceiling is cut across by a row of short semi-circular stalactites with pointed ends bearing a strange resemblance to a series of human female breasts. It is very probable that this resemblance did not escape the notice of the artists of Le Combel, for they smeared the stalactites with black. Similar discoveries have been made elsewhere, but, unlike the 'mother-goddesses' of Pech-Merle, the figures were invariably in open sites exposed to daylight. Examples are the bas-reliefs of Laussel, which are of astonishing realism; the nude female figures, their sexual characteristics carefully sculptured, of Angles-sur-Anglin and La Magdeleine (Tarn), and the reliefs with deeply engraved vulvas found at several sites in the Périgord. These representations may have had some connexion with maternity or love cults, but beyond that no explanation can be hazarded.

It must be pointed out that certain writers take a completely different view and interpret cave art in general as the manifestation, or a possible indication, of a primitive monotheism;† and indeed, if the hypothesis of totemism is incompatible with known facts and the theory of magic inadequate to provide a complete explanation, there is nothing at all to refute the argument that the magnificence of the underground sanctuaries indicates a religious significance. The writers advancing this theory maintain that it is confirmed by ethnographic data. It is based on the assumption that the conception of God is correlative with human intelligence, and indeed, as he was far

* Lemozi, *La Grotte-temple de Pech-Merle*, Paris, 1929.
† Th. Mainage, *Les Religions de la Préhistoire*, Paris, 1921, p. 438.

from being a creature of very limited intelligence, prehistoric man probably had conceived the idea of a God-Creator.

Examination of the Various Theories under Review

It is impossible to enter here into a detailed analysis of the various theories mentioned, or to attempt more than a general explanation why none of them can be considered as proved.

In spite of the diversity of their conclusions, the various writers (Mainage excepted) who have studied the significance of prehistoric wall art invariably show a similar approach to the subject. In an attempt to interpret it on the basis of present practices, they all seek to establish an affinity between the known facts relative to prehistoric art, and the rites and ceremonies practised by present-day primitive communities in connexion with beliefs apparently similar to those likely to have been held by Palaeolithic man. They select some object of prehistoric origin, such as a painting or an engraving, or some particular feature of wall art, and seek analogies to it within present-day communities believed to show some similarity to prehistoric man.

The deficiencies and uncertainties of comparative ethnographical methods are very apparent. They seek to make comparisons between archaeological data and heterogeneous communities with nothing in common save their classification as 'primitive peoples'. But the conception of 'primitive' is extremely difficult to define. There is much indiscriminate quoting of facts appertaining to communities which often differ greatly one from another and whose social, economic, or religious structures may be very different from those of prehistoric communities of which, in any case, practically nothing is known. For example, to explain the presence of masked figures in Palaeolithic art, the use of masks by Paleosiberians, Eskimoes, North American and South American Indians, Bushmen, Australian aborigines, the Shamans of Siberia, etc., has been cited. Some scholars interpret the Palaeolithic masked figures as men wearing hunting masks such as are worn by Bushmen; others make references to North American Indians and believe the Palaeolithic figures to represent participants in sacred dances; others again see in them the representation of a very ancient form of totemism analogous to the totem cult of Australian tribes; and yet others suppose them to represent gods, spirits, or mythical ancestors, etc. These differences in themselves prove the inadequacy of comparative ethnographical methods.

It is essential to know whether the comparisons made between a variety of dissimilar communities are all equally valid, after which the degree of validity of each comparison must be determined. It is generally considered that the more a characteristic is widespread throughout diverse communities, the greater its antiquity and the more fundamental its nature. When one particular characteristic is found to be common to every known primitive community, it is generally accepted as legitimate to attribute it to prehistoric man also if there is any archaeological material to support this conclusion. No one has ever seriously repudiated the existence of magical practices in Palaeolithic times, because such practices are universal, and, in addition, there is archaeological evidence to suggest their existence.

But universal characteristics are rare and beliefs and rituals many and varied. For example, the belief in semi-human beings is prevalent in numerous primitive communities, although its significance varies from one community to another. The use of masks or disguises may be linked to this belief, but in the circumstances these is no justification for comparing the semi-human beings represented in Palaeolithic cave art with those of one community rather than with those of another. A particular characteristic cannot be isolated from its setting; it does not exist as a separate entity, and comparisons between prehistoric and existing beliefs or rites are valid only to the extent that all the facts relevant to both correspond exactly. The data for Palaeolithic times are limited. Considerable information concerning existing primitive communities is available, but there is a lack of systematically compiled inventories; and, on a universal basis, we know almost nothing of any connexions which may exist between artistic manifestations and the beliefs which inspired them. Such inventories are essential. They need consist of only a limited category of artistic manifestations – for example, portrayals of composite animals, sexual organs, or animal-headed human figures, etc. – provided that they include all the known details of that particular category and, of course, show their correlation with the beliefs and ceremonies which inspired them. The validity of any particular comparison can be estimated only by means of such inventories, but unfortunately none exists. The use of comparative ethnographical methods in prehistory is inadequate because of the lacunae in the science of ethnology itself.

In the present state of our knowledge the only reasonably certain conclusions which comparative ethnography provides are of a very general nature, and relate to the preoccupation of primitive peoples with the sacred. This preoccupation is so universal (the only exceptions are to be found in Western communities), and prehistoric evidence so conclusive, that there is no reason to doubt that the attitude of the men who frequented the caves differed in any way on this point from that of men of historic times. There is likewise general agreement on the practice of sympathetic magic in prehistoric times, the basic elements of which are to be found in the practices of almost all known primitive communities. Apart from these general conclusions of far-reaching implication, comparative ethnography has not given any definite interpretation of the beliefs of prehistoric man. It has not revealed, for example, whether they were homogeneous or diverse, or whether they comprised the worship of gods, spirits, or mythical beings. It

has been equally unable to provide any clue to the rites and ceremonies which were the manifestations of these beliefs. In order
to progress beyond this preliminary stage of research without
hazarding any unverifiable theories, it is essential to be guided
by the existing archaeological evidence.

There has been too much haste to offer interpretations, to
put forward generalized hypotheses, and to seek explanations
outside the field of archaeology before compiling inventories
and collating all the archaeological evidence in order to extract
the utmost information from both sources. Apart from areas
of distribution, dating, and evolution, the study of which is
similar in essence whether applied to works of art or to any
other archaeological remains, there are three sources of information available for the study of the meaning of prehistoric
art. Firstly, the circumstances in which the work of art in
question was found; secondly, any signs of use which it may
show; thirdly, its form or content. These sources would seem
to provide all the information which could reasonably be
expected from an archaeological study of a work of art.

Position and association with other works and other remains are of great importance in the study of cave art. No
matter where an object such as a tool or a weapon may have
been lost, its position in a given stratigraphic layer links it to a
particular culture and helps to date it; but its position within
this layer is often the result of chance. The placing of works of
art in caves and on rock walls is, on the contrary, the result of
careful selection: the place where a painting or engraving is
found is undoubtedly the position *chosen* for it by the Palaeolithic artist. This fact is indisputable, and from it conclusions
of prime importance have been drawn. It is the position of the
paintings and engravings in the remotest parts of the caves
more than the figures themselves which immediately suggests
their magical or religious significance. In addition to the placing of a figure in a particular part of a cave, the positions of the
figures in relation to each other, the composition of a group,

the deliberate superpositions, the associations of one group of animals with another, or the association of signs and symbols with animals, etc., are of great significance. The study of these various associations has hitherto been more or less neglected. All objects found in the vicinity of a painting or an engraving – the broken spears or assegais found near the scene in the Shaft at Lascaux, the blades and flint blades found in the Gallery of Engravings in the same cave, for example – form part of the general context. The remains of a hearth, vestiges of cooking refuse, traces of human presence, or absence of such traces are all evidence which requires interpretation.

Marks of use on wall paintings or engravings are rare; such marks, however, are necessarily difficult to determine on material of ritual use, although they may be very clear on objects of material use. A ritual can, and generally does, consist of gestures, words, songs, etc., all of which leave no trace. In certain circumstances, however, some footmarks or other evidence of human presence near the representations, or marks of blows or signs of rubbing from human contact on the figures themselves, may be apparent. The bear of Montespan is a unique example.* Marks of blows which may have been made during ceremonies of sympathetic magic have also been reported on the painting of a small bison at Le Portel. A systematic study of the marks found in caves and on the paintings and engravings on their walls has never been attempted: it would, indeed, be a difficult task to accomplish, for it is not easy to distinguish accidental damage on a figure from deliberately inflicted scratches and scores. Engraved or painted darts cannot be considered as signs of use, for they do not appear to have been depicted after the completion of the animal figures; and, as a general rule, they have been very carefully executed in the

* A clay model probably representing the body of a bear was found at Montespan. In front of it lay the skull of a bear cub which was probably originally attached to it. The body of the model was covered with the marks of blows from a spear.

same technique as the figure on which they lie, or around which they are placed. In fact, they seem to have been conceived by the artist as an integral part of his composition in the same way as any other detail.* Paradoxically enough, it is the absence of any marks of use on most of the figures considered to be images of sympathetic magic which is most striking, and it is the absence or scarcity of signs of frequentation in caves which encourages the belief that ceremonies were of rare occurrence.

Thanks to its variety, the form of a representation – that is to say its content – is more enlightening and provides fundamental evidence of the artist's intentions. In this context, form or content includes not only the subject matter (animal or human figures, various signs, etc.) of a painting or engraving, but also the various characteristics of technique and style. These characteristics are vital for the chronological study of cave art, but they are of minor importance for the study of its meaning. The manner of representing any subject may vary from one generation to another but the reasons for its portrayal remain constant.†

The ideal approach to a study of the meaning of prehistoric cave art would be to prepare distribution maps according to the following criteria: position of the works in a cave, associated archaeological remains, signs of use, and content or form of a representation. Such maps would enable the various cultures exhibiting an assemblage of common traits to be grouped according to local distribution chronologically. Groups based on criteria of meaning might well differ from those based only on the evolution of style and technique, on which, up to the present, investigation has mainly been centred.

* Other marks which are often ignored in descriptions of the figures may be marks of use. Marks are numerous at Lascaux.

† Historically, the evolution of Christian art was far more rapid than the evolution of Christian beliefs. Cf. Henri Focillon, 'Préhistoire et Moyen Âge', *Dumbarton Oaks Papers*, Nos. 1, 2, and 3, November 1940, p. 4.

No significant trait can, however, be interpreted in isolation: each must be considered in its context. To study the masked figures, for example, by comparing them with other masked figures in the art of primitive cultures without first determining whether or not they are usually found in a particular part of a cave, or associated with particular animal species, or accompanied by signs, or rendered in a style different from that of other representations is to examine only one very limited aspect of the problem.

In archaeology there is always a tendency to look outside the archaeological record for the solution of a problem presented by the evidence; whereas, on the contrary, the archaeological material and all the known attendant circumstances should be exhaustively studied before any attempt is made to introduce comparisons with modern parallels, which is tantamount to introducing sources of error.

It would clearly be idle to suppose that the application of some rigid scheme of classification could supply the key to the riddle of cave art. All the beliefs and the mental outlook of Palaeolithic Man will never be completely revealed to us; the problem can only be closely examined, with no prospect of ever finding a complete solution. The compiling of an exhaustive inventory and a thorough study of all the details of each group of figures which might provide some clue to their meaning are immense tasks far outside the scope of a monograph on one cave, and in any case the results obtained might well be meagre.

All that has been attempted here is to give some guide to the manner in which such inventories might be compiled for the cave of Lascaux and to indicate a path which might lead to the discovery of a fresh interpretation of cave art more consistent with all the known facts.

CHAPTER 5

THE PURPOSE AND MEANING OF THE PAINTINGS AND ENGRAVINGS

THE conditions prevailing at Lascaux are particularly favourable to the study of the purpose and meaning of cave art. Although the superpositions are numerous, they are easier to decipher there than elsewhere; and, as most of the works are in a perfect state of preservation, they are less likely to be misinterpreted than those in other caves. All the requisite factors for the interpretation of cave art mentioned in the preceding chapter are present, and their careful study would provide a great deal of valuable information.

Marks and Signs of Use

The study of marks and traces of use on the paintings and engravings in a cave does not necessarily provide the key to their cause and meaning, but it does enable the problem to be approached more closely. It should comprise an investigation of the purposes for which a cave and each of its individual chambers may have been used, as well as of the uses to which individual paintings or groups of paintings may have been put. Only excavation can reveal the purpose and manner of a cave's use; the uses to which the works themselves were put can be determined only by excavation and the discovery of any marks which may have been made on them.

Incredible though it may seem, no serious excavation of the whole of a decorated cave has ever been undertaken. Hasty probings or partial excavations have been carried out in most caves, but there has never been any systematic attempt to find visible evidence of the passage of man in the various parts of the cave. Sometimes, in fact, traces which had remained undisturbed for thousands of years were destroyed by visitors too hastily invited by the discoverers, who trampled the floors without realizing the irreparable damage they were doing.* There has also been too much haste on the part of investigators to make trial probings without waiting for a systematic plan of excavation to be drawn up. It may well be, of course, that the great size of many chambers has discouraged any attempt at a comprehensive and thorough excavation. Perhaps the most harmful and dangerous step of all, however, has been the premature opening of caves to the public.

At Lascaux the equipment of the Great Hall of the Bulls was installed before any excavation had been undertaken, although the presence of charcoal in the clayey soil and a few human remains under the calcite in the bowl-like formations was an unmistakable sign that further discoveries might be made. The sub-soil of the chamber is still largely intact, but, if any large-scale excavations are ever undertaken, the cement path which follows the left-hand wall and the staircase at the entrance will prevent the collection of all the evidence which would have been accessible at the time of the discovery.

It is true that excavations in painted caves have generally been disappointing, but they have established one indisputable fact: the caves were not habitations, for the usual traces of human occupation (food refuse, fragments of various objects of human use, etc.) were absent. The remains found provide little evidence of the date of the site: they are often too scanty to be attributed with exactitude to any particular sub-division of Upper Palaeolithic. This lack of archaeological material may be another reason for the general reluctance to excavate

* The writer was able to visit the Galerie du Combel a few weeks after its discovery. The floor which had remained intact for thousands of years was already trampled; the bone fragments found scattered over the surface already collected and rearranged, and the passage leading to the small chamber in which the three fabulous animals are painted enlarged. All this was done before any systematic investigation had been made.

painted caves. Nevertheless, though it might yield none of the usual finds, a careful excavation of a cave floor would provide other valuable information.

A careful horizontal scraping of the soil would result in the exposure of one or more levels indicative of one or more periods of continuous or intermittent use of a cave. When Lascaux was discovered, certain parts of the floor may well have been the actual Palaeolithic floor, though in other places – the Great Hall of the Bulls, for example – some change had taken place. The original floor was covered over by thin deposits of limestone and clay, and a careful search for it under the few inches of deposit would have revealed it (except where it had been washed away by water) as it was when the last Palaeolithic Man left the cave. Perhaps certain features of the soil unnoticed when partial exploratory excavations in a cave are carried out would become apparent if a thorough examination were made. Even if no remains were found, an ancient floor much trodden by man or beast might be recognizable by its surface markings, the position of the elements strewn over it, and its blackened surface. Under it, other ancient floors similarly blackened and trampled might be uncovered.

Undoubtedly, the task of exposing the original floor of a cave is long and laborious, and the results achieved might well seem too meagre to justify all the exacting work involved. It is nevertheless of prime importance to determine the number of periods during which a cave was frequented; to establish whether these periods of frequentation coincide from one chamber to another; whether certain parts of the cave appear to have been more trodden, more frequented than others; and whether remains such as the spears or the handlamps in the Shaft at Lascaux are found in various parts of the cave or in certain special places only. If such excavations on a fairly large scale were undertaken, it would be infinitely better to concentrate all the available resources on the thorough investigation of an important site such as Lascaux than to spread them over several sites of secondary importance.

Other signs of frequentation are sometimes present besides those found on cave floors. Occasionally the walls of a cave are clearly worn by friction. At Lascaux, a stone which forms a sort of lip at the mouth of the Shaft of the Dead Man is both blackened and polished by the passage of human bodies: no other explanation seems possible. Similar polished stones have been found in other decorated caves; but it must be borne in mind that rubbing produces a polish comparatively quickly on limestone rock, and therefore it cannot be concluded with certainty that this effect can be produced only by the passage of human beings over a period of hundreds or thousands of years. Unfortunately, the reports on Lascaux issued at the time of its discovery made no mention of any trace of the passage of man on the vertical wall of the Shaft which might have explained the manner in which it was climbed; nor were any particular traces of human presence reported in the narrow corridor formed by the Chamber of Felines.

Some interesting conclusions in connexion with what is known or believed to be known of the practice of sympathetic magic in Palaeolithic times can be drawn from one particular sign of use. In some caves, quite apart from the representation of darts or other weapons, marks of blows which seem to have been deliberate have been found on certain figures. At Lascaux no such traces have been reported, but it would be of interest to re-examine the figures for their presence. In the Main Gallery there are two types of engraved line – one deep and clearly defined, which is used for the basic contour of the animals, the other a mere score on the limestone surface, a series of scratches rather than actual incisions, hasty and jerky strokes almost invariably straight. These are frequently found superposed on the engravings proper.

When copies of engravings are made, these light strokes are often ignored because they are so numerous and confused that their reproduction would interfere with the reading of the figures themselves. Nevertheless, it would be of interest to copy them and differentiate them from other strokes (by reproducing them in dotted line, for example) in order to determine their place, and possibly their purpose, in relation to the engravings generally. At Lascaux these strokes are very numerous in the Chamber of Engravings and the Chamber of Felines where there are networks of engravings. In addition, some slight scratches are visible on the walls around the engraved and painted panels in the central part of the Main Gallery. They look very fresh and clear, but it is possible that they are contemporaneous with the paintings and engravings. It may be that they were made accidentally when branches or weapons, for example, were handled inside the cave; or possibly they were made by missiles thrown in the course of ritual ceremonies.* It is particularly difficult to determine the purpose and origin of these marks because their connexion with the figures themselves is very uncertain.

The Position of the Paintings and the various Animal Groupings and Associations

It has hitherto been customary to study separately the individual figures depicted on the walls of caves. This piecemeal method has been used for the study of figures of similar style, which are probably contemporaneous, as well as superposed figures considered to belong to successive periods. Yet, as his works testify, Palaeolithic Man's visual reactions were very similar to our own, and he was well aware of the coherent effect of his creative achievements in the chambers and galleries of the caves. At Lascaux, composed groups are more strikingly apparent than in any other cave, and *a priori* there is

---

* It seems unlikely that these marks were made recently – for example, when the scaffolding for the taking of photographs was erected.

no reason to doubt that the various groups of one or several animal species depicted on the walls of underground sanctuaries were deliberately *composed* by Palaeolithic Man and that, far from being mere juxtapositions of one species with another, these compositions had a definite purpose. Despite its likelihood, however, this theory is not easy to prove.

Today the base of a painting or drawing (canvas, paper, etc.) is geometrically limited, and therefore the setting (landscape, for example) generally constitutes the unity of a picture. In Palaeolithic art a background is never depicted and evidence of the deliberate composition of a group is to be found in the arrangement of the different subjects in relation to each other, or in the repetition of groups of identical subjects from one panel to another or from one cave to another.

The simplest and clearest example of planned grouping is the frieze or an assemblage of a single species of animal depicted in one particular style. At Lascaux friezes are particularly numerous: there are some in almost every chamber, on almost every wall – the bulls of the Great Hall, the horses or heads of bovids in the Painted Gallery, the deer in the Chamber of Engravings, the swimming deer, and the files of painted and engraved horses in the Main Gallery, etc. (Plates 1, 4, 7, 12, etc.). Although they cannot properly be described as friezes, certain groups of animals like the two bistre wild asses, or the two bison shown back to back (Plate 41), were clearly the result of the same inspiration. It must not be assumed that each frieze at Lascaux is a mere repetition of one single subject, though it has sometimes been maintained that this is the case in other caves: there is clear evidence of planned composition in several instances where the outlines of a group were drawn in before any details were added. In the Great Hall, for example, the unfinished sketches at each end of the frieze of bulls which are harmoniously arranged in a semi-circle, the hindquarters of one covered by the forequarters of another, prove that this design was carefully planned and composed.

The two horses (Plate 31) galloping shoulder to shoulder which are shown emerging from the croup of the large cow in the Main Gallery provide an even more striking example of deliberate composition. One is painted in red, the other in brown, and the artist has limited the two areas of colour with precision; the overlapping of one by the other conforms strictly to our own rules of composition. In addition, the almost symmetrical arrangement of the two bison shown back to back is clear evidence that this group also was most carefully composed.

These facts are obvious, and they are important. The theory now generally accepted that the purpose of Palaeolithic cave art was the practice of sympathetic magic is based on the supposition that the figures were painted one at a time according to the needs of the hunt. It might well be supposed, however, that groups of animals were portrayed by Palaeolithic Man for purposes of sympathetic magic rather than individual specimens, for this would correspond to a desire for an abundance of game. This supposition is not wholly unacceptable, but it is not satisfactory, since it does not take all the facts into account. It provides no explanation, for example, of the two male bison shown back to back, or the frieze of bulls facing each other in the Great Hall. Almost all Palaeolithic caves contain similar paintings of groups of animals of the same species shown back to back, facing each other, in files, or in confusion, and an inventory of all such groups should be compiled for purposes of comparison.

A study of processions of animals of the same species or of the same sex is a simple matter, whereas the study of groups of animals of various species is more complex, because it is difficult to determine whether their association is deliberate or fortuitous. Several instances can be cited. Sometimes the figures are merely juxtaposed – for example, the leaping cow and the group of small horses surrounding it – and the only way to determine whether or not the juxtaposition is deliberate is to establish whether that particular association of cow and horse is especially frequent on the panels of Lascaux or other caves; sometimes they overlap each other, and in these instances the pattern of the encroachment may indicate whether it is accidental or deliberate.

It is strikingly apparent at Lascaux that some of the earliest figures are almost completely masked by superpositions, although in some cases parts of the contours were utilized for later figures. The large black bull (Fig. 13) of the Painted Gallery which covers four heads of bistre bovids and two red cows is the clearest example of such a superposition. Other black or red painted animals cover earlier figures of cervids.* The fact that for some unknown reason an early figure was not utilized, but was carefully covered by another perhaps more in accordance with the taste of the period, may be attributable to purely aesthetic considerations. It is not inconceivable, however, that in some cases the superpositions may have had some deeper significance.

On several occasions it has been reported that one of the large bulls (Plate 1 and Fig. 21) in the Great Hall is superposed on another earlier one outlined in red. From a careful examination of the two outlines, however, it would seem that in actual fact the red lines protruding below the black ones do not continue underneath them, but end abruptly. Deterioration cannot be the cause of this sudden break, since the line is very clear, neither blurred nor faded: the underlying red bovid was evidently never completed.

In these circumstances, contrary to general belief, it would seem unlikely that the large bull painted in black bands is a reconstruction of a red animal of earlier date. The red lines either belong to an incomplete sketch slightly modified by the

* Breuil and Glory have reported some cervids beneath the black horse of Fig. 14, beneath the red bovids in the same Gallery, and beneath the large black cow in the Main Gallery. These cervids are difficult to decipher and the writer was not able to discover them.

black outline, a suggestion which is not at variance with what is known of the various techniques used in many of the works at Lascaux, or else the superposition was intentional and part of a preconceived composition. But why should a black bull have been placed over a red one, almost completely hiding it? The conclusion that the superposition was deliberate would further complicate the problem. In fact, no conclusion at all can be drawn from this example, which up to the present is unique.*

Black superpositions over red are generally found on animals of the same species. Other curious superpositions or juxtapositions of horses and bovids sometimes occur, however, and it is possible that these are not all due to chance. The bison and the horse (probably a mare) painted and engraved at the junction of the Lateral Passage and the Main Gallery provide the clearest example of planned juxtaposition (Fig. 16); they are of similar technique and are unquestionably contemporaneous. The careful arrangement of the figures, which are shown back to back, their hindquarters symmetrically superposed, is clearly apparent. This arrangement is by no means unique in Palaeolithic art. At Lascaux the two bison shown back to back are similarly designed, and at Pech-Merle there is an identical grouping of two stippled horses (Plate 38). It is very possible that this arrangement of the figures was not designed for mere stylistic effect.

In actual fact, animals of the same species live together, and a bison and a horse side by side can hardly have been a common sight for the Palaeolithic hunter. In an art so realistic this strange juxtaposition is inexplicable, but it is a fact that such groupings of horse and bovid are very frequent at Lascaux and

---

* Other superpositions of black over red have been reported at Lascaux, but these may merely correspond to a 'vogue' for black, following an earlier 'vogue' for red. Several red animals (a horse and some bovids) have been touched up and completed in black. It is not easy to determine whether these black re-touchings are contemporary with the paintings or definitely later in date, but the present hypothesis seems the more likely one.

elsewhere. An inventory of such juxtapositions is difficult to compile, because there is a risk of confusing deliberate with fortuitous groupings. The planned composition of some of these groups, however, is indisputable.

The deliberate juxtaposition of horse and bison occurs in two paintings at Lascaux. In one of them three animals depicted in wide red bands appear to be emerging from the tunnel at the end of the Painted Gallery. They are all undoubtedly contemporaneous. A male bison (Plate 16) leads the way; a horse follows, then another animal, probably a horse too. The three figures are juxtaposed, but there is no superposition. The other painting at the junction of the Lateral Passage and the Main Gallery is of later date and portrays the bison and horse in superposition already mentioned, together with five other horses. These figures form a harmonious composition arranged on two planes; two horses are represented on the lower plane, and at each end of the upper plane, which is separated from the lower one by a projection of the rock face, a latticed sign is painted. The bison is pierced by seven darts and is shown advancing towards the sign on the right; the three horses, two of them also pierced by darts, are advancing towards the sign on the left. The deliberate composition of the scene is clear (see Fig. 15).

In the Great Hall of the Bulls the horses almost invariably appear to have been painted after the bovids (oxen in this case) with which they are associated. A deliberate association of horse and bovid is not clearly apparent in this chamber.

In both the Painted Gallery and the Main Gallery the association of horse and bovid is more clearly defined. The grouping of the red-and-black cows and the bistre-and-black horses on the vault and the walls of the Painted Gallery (Plates 7, 9, and 10) can scarcely be regarded as fortuitous. A certain symmetry is immediately apparent between the two figures on the left wall of this Gallery – the large black bull (Plate 18) and the black horse facing in opposite directions (Plate 13), each advancing towards a branched black sign. The leaping cow on the right-hand wall and some, at least, of the small horses surrounding it would seem to form a complete picture (Plate 12). The large cow (Plate 30) on the left-hand wall of the Main Gallery with its legs entangled in latticed signs has evidently been deliberately superposed on several painted and engraved horses, although it is impossible to judge whether this superposition was intended merely to mask earlier works, or if it has some mythical or historical significance which we cannot fathom.

These data are too scanty, too insubstantial, for any conclusion to be drawn from them. Some of the associations are probably fortuitous, but the mere fact that one, at least (the bison and the mare back to back), is undoubtedly deliberate is sufficient to raise a problem which has hitherto never been considered at all. If an inventory of these animal associations in other caves as well as those at Lascaux were compiled, it is possible that certain factors common to all of them might be revealed. Associations which are not fortuitous are undoubtedly present in other caves besides Lascaux.

Numerous photographs have been published of one of the main panels at Pech-Merle portraying mammoths, bovids, bison, and horses painted in black line and attributed to Early Magdalenian. On the left of this panel a mammoth is depicted either in close proximity to a slender bovid, or possibly slightly superposed on it (Plate 36). The two figures have always been studied separately, and the possibility of their deliberate association has never been considered; but two sketches on the wall near this group show that it is undoubtedly a deliberate composition, for they are almost identical: each portrays the back of a mammoth crossed by an undulating line which is clearly the back of another animal (Plate 37). Both sketches, which were left unfinished for some unknown reason, prove that the design of the mammoth was conceived at the same time as the design of the other animal.

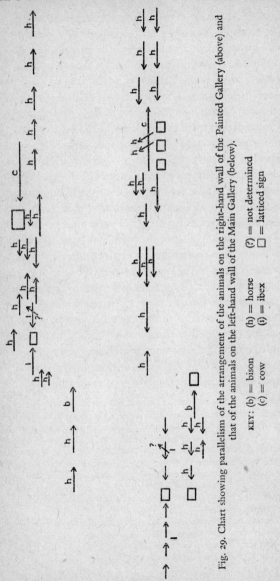

Fig. 29. Chart showing parallelism of the arrangement of the animals on the right-hand wall of the Painted Gallery (above) and that of the animals on the left-hand wall of the Main Gallery (below).

KEY: (b) = bison   (h) = horse   (?) = not determined
       (c) = cow   (i) = ibex   □ = latticed sign

This fact is sufficient evidence that the Palaeolithic artists depicted carefully composed groups of animals, and that many closely associated figures *which have hitherto been interpreted as juxtapositions or superpositions should in fact be regarded as deliberately planned compositions.*

Nevertheless, there is a wide gap to be bridged before any conclusions regarding a new interpretation of prehistoric wall art can be drawn from this evidence. The first and most indispensable step towards this end is the compiling of detailed inventories for each period and for each cave. However, it is not inadmissible to speculate on the possible results of the discovery of numerous repetitions of particular animal associations. It might be revealed, for example, that the Palaeolithic friezes depict legends or myths of very great antiquity. Perhaps the left-hand panel of the Main Gallery (Plate 30) at Lascaux might be a repetition in a slightly different form of the right-hand panel of the Painted Gallery (Plate 12). The central subject is the same: a large black bovid advancing towards the back of the cave. On one panel the animal appears to be leaping towards a latticed sign; on the other, its two hindlegs and its tail are entangled in three similar signs. One bovid is surrounded by some seventeen painted horses, the other by about twenty, both painted and engraved, some of which it masks completely.* If similar compositions consisting of numerous

---

* The analogy can perhaps be pursued still further. To the left of each of these panels, animals of similar species are depicted. In the Painted Gallery two ibexes of different colour are separated by a latticed sign; in the Main Gallery there are two groups of ibex heads of different colour and between them a four-sided, very lightly engraved sign. In both Galleries a bison and some horses are depicted slightly below the other figures. There is yet another similarity, insignificant but puzzling; a small red figure (a horse?) is painted across the back of one of the ibexes of the Painted Gallery, and an indeterminate shape (antelope, female ibex) is engraved over one of the groups of ibex heads in the Main Gallery (Fig. 29).

In contrast with these analogies, there are many dissimilarities in the number of animals, their attitudes, and their respective positions. The resemblance between the two panels is none the less noteworthy.

Should it be proved that these groups are in fact compositions, fresh diffi-

animal figures are found in other caves, the hypothesis of realistic scenes being ruled out, it may be that these paintings represent the oldest surviving narratives of mankind.

There are, however, a few instances of groups of varied animal species which may depict actual scenes from life. The group of lions in the Chamber of Felines, for example, is associated with some horses. Such associations are of frequent occurrence in wall art: there are other examples at Font-de-Gaume and at Pech-Merle in the Gallery of Le Combel. They may, of course, merely represent groups of horses attacked by felines. If, however, some of the animal associations are regarded as mythical scenes, it would seem that the ensemble of the works in the cave should be similarly interpreted.

Other valuable information may be gathered from the position of the figures in the different parts of a cave. It is very probable that the Quaternary artists did not place their works at random on the rock-face. Why should a figure drawn on the vast wall of a large chamber have the same significance as another hidden between two projections of rock far from the main chambers and difficult to find? Was the inaccessible spot selected merely for difficulty's sake, or was there some other reason for the choice?

A hypothesis has been put forward that the paintings and engravings in caves are related to a belief that animals were born in the bowels of the earth and reached the outer world by means of underground galleries and tunnels. It is an attractive supposition which would explain the abundance of the various species represented in cave art and also why prehistoric artists

---

culties would arise, for all the figures belonging to one composition must obviously be of the same date. According to Breuil's classification, the panel of the leaping cow at Lascaux belongs to five or six different periods; in the simplified classification set out on pp. 109–10 it belongs rather to the first three phases of the cave's decoration. If either of these technical and stylistic classifications is correct, then the theory of deliberate compositions is no longer tenable.

so often chose a natural hollow or projection of the rock-face on which to portray their animals, for thus they appear to be born from the very rock itself.* Nevertheless, the theory is unsatisfactory. To give it validity, all the animals should be facing the same way towards the exterior of the cave and the light of day, which is not the case. Furthermore, it provides no explanation of the animals pierced by darts, or the concentration of certain species or certain signs in particular parts of the cave.

Another fact worthy of study and classification is that the geometrical signs are sometimes found scattered among the figures on the walls of caves and sometimes concentrated in particular places, usually remote and difficult of access. Such concentrations are very noticeable at Lascaux. Apart from the latticed signs in the chambers and galleries, there are two groups of signs: one is engraved in the Chamber of Felines, the other inside the small dome (Plate 23) over the mouth of the Shaft.

Two of these signs and four parallel engraved lines which are undoubtedly associated with them can be deciphered in the Chamber of Felines; and two identical groups of four lines

---

* However the position of the paintings may have been explained hitherto, there is no doubt that the actual surface of the rock must often have suggested the silhouette of an animal to the Palaeolithic artist. A continual preoccupation arising out of a variety of circumstances (for example, the constant desire of the hunters for game) leads to the formation of images relative to it. This is the principle of the test devised by Rorschach which consists in describing ten different inkspots – five black, two black and red, three multi-coloured. Each individual, according to his particular occupation or anxieties, sees a different image in the same inkspot, and his interpretation is considered to indicate the mental or emotional type to which he belongs. Children form images with much more facility than adults; they see shapes in the patterns or marks on wallpaper in their rooms, in clouds in the sky, etc. The natural curves of the rock, the bosses, the hollows, the stalactites, and the variations of colour in the world underground conjure up an extraordinary variety of animal shapes – croups, legs, necks, shoulders, etc. In the silence of the cave, the flickering light of a handlamp intensifies the illusions; and if but a day is spent in the study of the Palaeolithic paintings a whole world of fauna of infinite variety of form and movement will seem to come to life. On the Palaeolithic hunters the effect of the cave must have been even more powerful.

have been engraved on the left and on the right of the cupola over the Shaft. Beyond it, three latticed signs are visible. Two of them are polychrome; they are divided into sections painted in different colours, and are very similar to those placed under the feet of the large cow in the Gallery of Engravings; the third is engraved only.

A noteworthy fact which requires explanation is the similarity between the signs in the Chamber of Felines and those in the cupola. In both places one sign is edged with fine parallel hatchings, one section of another scored or scratched all over, and each is preceded by four parallel lines accompanied by a very long undulating band hatched with short engraved or painted transverse strokes formed in part by a natural vein in the rock. No reason can be given for the similarity of these two groups, but it is clear that it is not fortuitous. In addition, tracings made by Abbé Glory (which are not yet published) show a lioness's head in the Chamber of Engravings close to the cupola. Does this represent yet another similarity to the Chamber of Felines?

Each of the two groups of latticed signs indicates or gives warning of a vertical drop of several feet. A bison's head is painted on the wall of one of these steep drops. The scene of the bird-headed man (Plate 35) at the bottom of the other and the site itself bespeaks the importance the Palaeolithic hunters attached to this painting. As no comparable scene exists in Palaeolithic art, no explanation can be given for its extraordinary situation at the bottom of a deep shaft at the junction of several clayey fissures.

The concentration of signs in particular spots is correlative to the accumulation of figures on other parts of the rock-face. The medley of engravings in the Chamber of Engravings is not a phenomenon peculiar to Lascaux alone: such networks are found in several caves, but Les Trois Frères provides the most striking example. A comparative study of these concentrations has yet to be made.

A study of the situation of the figures, the position of one in relation to another, the recurrence of certain groupings from one wall to another or from one cave to another can show whether the association of the figures was deliberate or fortuitous. The results of such an inevitably long study which it has been possible only to outline here and which should embrace all the known wall paintings and engravings dating from the same period may well be meagre; nevertheless, such an analysis is the first essential step towards the discovery of the meaning of prehistoric wall art.

The Subject Matter of the Paintings and Engravings and its Connexion with Hunting Magic

The subject matter of the paintings and engravings provides more information than anything else about the thoughts, desires, and possibly the beliefs of the Palaeolithic hunters. Their interests do not appear to have been very varied: indeed it would seem that they were entirely focused on the hunt and the quarry. Most of the animals represented are edible and, from the evidence of bone remains found on the sites, they did, in fact, provide the staple food of the period. The enemies of man and the quarry he hunted – the felines, for example, whose flesh is not edible – are less frequently depicted: the comparative ratio is about 1 to 50 or 100 (at Lascaux there are six or seven felines to about 200 horses, bovids, etc.), which accords well with the theory of the magic purpose of the figures. Attempts to make the theory of sympathetic magic agree in detail with the known facts, however, reveal so many inconsistencies that its inadequacy is immediately apparent. For example:

1. The representation of animals of various species in files or in groups cannot have corresponded to the actual desires of the hunters. It is surely impossible to interpret the pike painted

along the back of one of the horses at Pech-Merle, or the horse and the bison with superposed croups at Lascaux, to mention only two indisputable examples of grouping, as images for the practice of sympathetic magic.

2. The imaginary animals and the semi-human figures are also incompatible with the theory of sympathetic magic; and the theory that they represent hunting masks or have some connexion with ritual hunting dances seems untenable to the writer. Present-day primitive peoples use hunting masks in order to approach the animals they wish to kill without awakening their suspicions, but the Palaeolithic human figures bear little resemblance to masked hunters. At Cougnac and Pech-Merle they are little creatures with heads vaguely reminiscent of a bird's, and their bodies are pierced with darts; at Lascaux the bird-headed man appears to be dead or wounded; and at Les Trois Frères the 'sorcerer' bearing large antlers, whose general appearance is certainly more like that of a man in disguise, looks down on the medley of engraved animals below him. There is nothing about any of these figures to suggest a masked being seeking to approach his quarry unseen.

The theory of hunting dances is not wholly unacceptable, but there is no apparent link between these dances, the figures depicted in the caves, and the hunting activities of a tribe. It is difficult to understand how the bird-headed man and the bird perched on a stake at his feet, for example, could further the success of the hunt. In fact, no explanation at all can be hazarded until fresh evidence is discovered, or an interpretation more consistent with the actual facts is put forward. Such an interpretation should take into account a statement once made by Luquet which has almost invariably been ignored.

'When considering prehistoric art, reality is often confused with the image. The actual performance of a masked dance is very different from the portrayal of a masked being, the efficacy of the dance very different from the efficacy of the image. There is no point in portraying a ceremony which can be performed in reality.'* Why should the sorcerers, who were probably the artists of the tribe, depict themselves on the walls of the sanctuary wearing their masks? The semi-human beings and the imaginary animals cannot be explained merely by the theory of sympathetic magic: it seems more likely that they represent mythical beings who were perhaps connected in some way with the history of the ancestors of the group.

3. The majority of the animals depicted in cave art are shown in peaceful attitudes with no sign of any wound or any deadly weapon. At Lascaux, for example, only one of a total number of nine horses in the Hall of the Bulls appears to have a dart plunged in its head; and of a total of seven bovids only one is shown with a hooked dart embedded in its muzzle. The six deer bear no mark of any kind. It is true that large red or black dots and the various signs which have never been interpreted might represent weapons or wounds (Plates 5, 6, etc.); but, even if they did, the number of animals conforming to the classic theory of sympathetic magic would still remain very limited. This theory must therefore be modified and the portrayal of non-wounded animals regarded merely as a means of ensuring the presence or an abundance of game in the region; or else rites of sympathetic magic must be considered to consist merely of gestures and incantations in front of images without any marks being made on them thereby. There is nothing to refute these hypotheses, but there is likewise nothing to support them.

The interpretation of the signs is closely linked to the theory of the magic purpose of Palaeolithic art. If all, or nearly all, the signs can be identified as weapons, the theory of sympathetic

* Luquet, *L'Art et la religion des hommes fossiles*, Paris, 1926, p. 229, Fig. 129; and 'La magie dans l'art paléolithique', *Journal de Psychologie*, 1931, pp. 390–427.

magic is reinforced though not proved; if they represent other objects – tribal emblems or unidentifiable symbols – then this theory must be made more comprehensive and flexible, or even perhaps discarded. Here again the study of one cave alone cannot solve the problem: only a study of inventories and comparisons embracing wall art as a whole can provide an answer. In these pages it has only been possible to put forward a few suggestions relative to Lascaux alone.

The signs painted and engraved on the walls of the cave can be divided into several categories. First of all, there are the *various weapons* which can be identified with some degree of assurance: *darts*, painted or engraved; *assegais*, and even *harpoons*. Darts and all the other signs are more numerous at Lascaux in the later phases of its artistic development and can be identified without difficulty. A great number are depicted by a straight line with two short slanting strokes at each side of one end (Plate 28a) and are very similar to modern representations of arrows. In some instances, however, only one of these short strokes is shown (Plate 6); and these signs probably represent another type of weapon. The fletching (?) of some of the darts is carefully depicted: for example, it is seen on those placed around the bistre-and-black horse of Plate 10. Other weapons are depicted by a straight line only (Plate 12), and others again by lines with various bifurcations (Plates 7 and 9) which may represent the bone assegais frequently found on the sites.

The method of propelling these various missiles is not known; no bow has ever been discovered on the sites and none is represented in any way in Franco-Cantabrian art. It is believed that Palaeolithic man possessed the spear-thrower – a weapon still used by certain South American tribes – for engraved bones with a hooked end have often been discovered in Upper Palaeolithic sites. It is generally agreed that the hooked stick painted at the feet of the bird-headed man is a spear-thrower (Plate 35), the two short transverse lines at the opposite end to the hook being the butt.★

The engraved harpoons on the vault of the Chamber of Engravings † present a particular problem with regard to dating. Most Palaeolithic bone harpoons have been discovered on sites dating from Middle Magdalenian ‡ onwards; and, if the harpoons engraved in the Chamber of Engravings are of earlier date than the Magdalenian period, they provide additional evidence that the interval between the Late Perigordian and Early Magdalenian paintings and engravings was comparatively short.

The remaining signs are more difficult to identify. They include the multi-branched stems placed in front of the large black horse of Plate 13 or the bull of Plate 18; the two parallel lines with a smaller perpendicular line crossing one of them shown in front of a small incomplete polychrome horse in the Hall of the Bulls § and one of the bistre-and-black horses in the Painted Gallery (Plate 10). In one instance this sign is placed in front of the animal's nostrils, and in the other in front of its neck; the perpendicular line of one sign points towards it, that of the other away from it. No explanation of these signs has ever been put forward. There are also other signs composed of lines arranged in various patterns which are equally puzzling. The presence of these signs in other caves and the circumstances in which they are found should be investigated.

In the Chamber of Engravings there is an attractive engraving of a deer pierced by a clearly defined dart. In the area of

★ It is probable that there is some relation between the spear-thrower, the bird-headed man, the bird perched on a stave, and the bone spear-thrower decorated with a sculptured bird's head found at Mas d'Azil.

† Reported by Abbé Glory.

‡ Some harpoon prototypes in reindeer horn have, however, been found in the Upper Perigordian levels in the Chasseur shelter at Vilhonneur (Charente). Cf. L'Anthropologie, 1939–40, pp. 697–701.

§ Fernand Windels, The Lascaux Cave Paintings, 1949, p. 79.

its shoulder a sign has been painted in a purplish-red rare at Lascaux and used only for filling-in certain sections of poly-chrome latticed signs. This mace-like sign is somewhat re-miniscent of the claviforms in the Pyrenean caves, but it is the only example at Lascaux.

Punctuations, on the contrary, are numerous at Lascaux and indeed in Palaeolithic art generally. They consist of large red or black discs more or less uniform in size and with a diameter of approximately 4–6 in. As a general rule they are painted in rows, but sometimes they are shown singly. Their outlines are generally blurred and the artists appear to have formed them by blowing the pigments on to the walls. In common with other signs, these punctuations seem to have some particular connexion with animals: they are often associated with deer (Plate 11). In other caves (La Galerie du Combel at Pech-Merle, for example), punctuations of similar type are shown in isola-tion and unconnected with any other figure. They have some-times been interpreted as marks to signpost the alleys of under-ground sanctuaries, but this interpretation is unacceptable in the case of Lascaux, for there the punctuations are invariably found on the painted panels and there could have been no danger of getting lost in the cave.

Yet a further type of sign peculiar to Lascaux consists of long sinuous lines, sometimes branched, which are usually de-scribed as 'creepers'. Two of these signs are painted in dark ochre at the end of the Painted Gallery close to the horse fall-ing backwards (Plate 15), another is painted in the Chamber of Felines, and yet another engraved in the dome over the Shaft. (These last two signs have been described on pages 76 and 94.) A fifth, long and undulating, is carefully engraved on one wall of the Chamber of Engravings. With its central stem and multitude of slanting and parallel lines at each side, it resembles a gigantic feather. It is very unlikely, however, that this is its correct interpretation; like the other signs, it is most probably some form of 'creeper' though it might be interpreted as a type of hunting weapon – a lasso, perhaps, to catch the animals.

Finally, there are the 'hut' signs formed by a cluster of engraved lines spreading out from a central point towards the base. These signs have several times been reported in Palaeolithic art; they are particularly noticeable at Altamira, and there are three of them in the Chamber of Engravings at Lascaux (Plate 25). It has been suggested that they represent sorcerers enveloped in a disguise of dried grass; but this interpretation is not convincing, for the 'face' is formed by irregularities of the rock and bears no trace of human handiwork.

The latticed signs at Lascaux have aroused widespread interest. Signs of a similar type have been found in other decorated caves in France and Spain, but possibly no other cave contains so many which are both homogeneous and varied. There are about thirty of these signs at Lascaux; some are painted, some engraved, and some both painted and engraved. They are usually four-sided, divided lengthwise into three sections and crosswise into two. Two short parallel strokes are often engraved or painted at the end of one or more of the sections, but there are numerous variations of this design: hatchings on the edges or in the central part, scorings, variations in the arrangement of the sections, variations in the colours, etc. (Fig. 24). In the main, however, only the contours are engraved or painted, and the interior of the sections is filled in with scorings and sometimes with solid colour. The three signs accompanying the large cow in the Gallery of Engravings (Fig. 25) and those in the dome of the Chamber of Engravings have been depicted in a special manner. Each section has been carefully painted in a different colour from that of the adjacent sections; so every sign usually shows four colours. In several instances mauves and purplish-reds, very rare colours in Palaeolithic art, have been used for these sections.

Latticed signs are more numerous in the engraved chambers than in the painted ones; there is not one in the Hall of the Bulls. They seem to be placed in a particular position in relation to the animals they accompany. As a general rule they are placed in front of an animal, rarely behind it, and sometimes they are placed on its body.

There is no general agreement on the interpretation to be given to these signs. Similar signs in other caves are frequently triangular in shape and at first were thought to be 'huts'. Subsequently, it was suggested that they might be traps – some kind of pitfall to ensnare large game (Plate 47) or perhaps a type of weighted trap like those used by many hunting peoples today. The polychrome signs at Lascaux have sometimes been described as blazons or tribal emblems.

The interpretation of the signs at Lascaux as 'huts' is unacceptable: both their shape and their position rule out this explanation. On the other hand, the theory that they represent traps is feasible on account of their position in relation to the animals; but the type of trap would have to be determined and the meaning of the details so carefully depicted explained. The theory of tribal emblems is also a likely one, because the geometrical designs differ from one cave to another; but it would make the connexion of the signs with the animals incomprehensible. A wholly satisfactory interpretation of these signs has still to be found.

The most widely accepted theory – the theory of sympathetic magic – would thus appear to be untenable as far as the cave of Lascaux is concerned. The absence of any traces of sympathetic magic, the existence of animal associations bearing no relation to the natural associations in real life of the animals hunted, the presence of signs unlike any kind of weapon, the strange composite animal near the entrance, the bird-headed man of the Shaft, all argue against this theory. A similar argument could be put forward in almost identical terms in the case of many of the other painted caves belonging to the Franco-Cantabrian group.

CONCLUSION

THE various problems presented by the cave of Lascaux are far from being solved; the paintings and engravings cannot yet be attributed with certainty to any particular phase of the Upper Palaeolithic, and the superpositions set out in sequence in these pages present perplexing difficulties.

The view that the cave as a whole constitutes a single unity and that each artist who worked there placed his figures in relation to those already existing is inconsistent with belief in an evolution of the artistic techniques used; and even though various associations and compositions may be established, the problem of their meaning has still to be solved. In fact, the meaning of the cave as a whole remains obscure. In spite of the immense progress made since the early discoveries at the end of the ninteenth century the underground world of Palaeolithic art has not yet revealed all its secrets.

An important step forward would be taken if these underground paintings and engravings were to be studied anew from the standpoint of deliberate associations and compositions, and their interpretation as myths of great antiquity confirmed.

With each new discovery it becomes more amd more apparent that the meaning of cave art must not be sought in a study of single figures; on the contrary, individual figures which have hitherto been photographed or copied and studied outside their context must be re-integrated into the panel to which they belong, and possibly each panel considered as an integral part of the cave and its decorated chambers as a whole. This new method of studying Palaeolithic art will enable the dominant motives inspiring the paintings and engravings in each cave or region to be recognized.

The *first* step is not to establish whether a particular geometric sign represents a hut or a trap, or a certain animal-headed figure a masked hunter on the basis of a few remote ethnographic comparisons, or whether a particular animal shown pierced by a dart was used in a ritual of sympathetic magic, for the evidence is too scanty for any such conclusions to be drawn; the *essential preliminary* is the singling out of the main subjects and associations which inspired the cave artists, and this is a comparatively simple task involving little risk of error.

At Lascaux, the subject matter of some of the paintings or engravings is evident: the association of bison and horse, for instance, or horse and cow – possibly bull and cow – and the association of these animals with latticed signs. Latticed signs are also found in proximity to the lions and the only rhinoceros in the cave – both dangerous species very different from the bovids, horses, caprids and cervids mainly represented on the walls – and would thus appear to have some particular significance. Other latticed signs are placed in groups at far ends of the cave above deep pits. The association of horse and bovid is found in a number of Palaeolithic paintings and engravings. In certain examples of *art mobilier* and in certain sculptures of South-Western France this association is sometimes replaced by that of bison and woman (Angles-sur-Anglin, Laussel, La Magdeleine). We are unable to interpret this theme, but it is obvious that it was important in the minds of the Palaeolithic artists. Various forms of latticed signs are present in the majority of painted caves; their associations and the circumstances in which they are found are similar from the Dordogne to Spain, and they are undoubtedly of the same significance.

The bird-headed man in the Shaft at Lascaux and the composite fabulous animal of the Great Hall of the Bulls are subjects present in other caves besides Lascaux – particularly Pech-Merle. Like the dangerous animals, they seem, in these two caves, to be quite distinct from the central panels which, at Lascaux, are mainly composed of horses and bovids and, at Pech-Merle, of horses, bovids and mammoths. Here again each figure must be re-integrated into the cave's decoration as a whole and the idea of a hierarchy or the existence of some unknown relationship between the individual figures considered.

There are numerous and striking parallelisms between the subjects, the associations and the disposition of the Lascaux paintings and engravings and those of other Palaeolithic caves; and, since none of these associations are of a natural order, the theory of an anecdotal animal art is ruled out. In these pictorial descriptions the artist has either given free rein to his imagination on the basis of traditional themes or else he has perpetuated on the walls of caves legends of remote antiquity. In both cases the unvarying nature of subjects common to widely dispersed human groups is significant.

It is still far too early, however, to attempt to explain the nature of these themes. Do they represent the order of the universe and the relationship between one living creature and another, or do they portray a sequence of events? Do they illustrate myths concerning the origin of man, the lives of supernatural beings, or death and the after-life? No definitive answer can be given. Though the friezes of Lascaux and other caves may suggest a world where animals and their relationships played an all-important part whilst man was no more than an intruder and a victim, yet we have no conception of the place this world may have held in the mind of Palaeolithic man.

Although we are unable to interpret the themes of these underground paintings and engravings, their very existence proves that the mentality of Palaeolithic man was far more complex than is generally supposed and that the scope of his artistic inspiration extended far beyond a daily preoccupation with the hunt and its quarry. If these paintings and engravings do indeed illustrate myths of very great antiquity, they may represent man's first attempt to express his vision of the world and the relationship of one living creature with another.

BIBLIOGRAPHY

BARGHOORN, Elso S. et MOVIUS Jr. Hallam L., 'Lascaux charcoal'. *Sciences*, vol. 114, 1951, n. 2961, p. 333.

BATAILLE, Georges, *Lascaux, ou la naissance de l'art*. Genève, 1955.

BATE, M. A. Dorothea, 'The "Licorne" of Lascaux: is it Pantholops?', *The Archaeological News Letters*, vol. 2, no. 11, 1950, pp. 182–4.

BLANC, Séverin, 'Grotte de Lascaux, commune de Montignac-sur-Vézère (Dordogne)', *Gallia*, fouilles et monuments archéologiques en France métropolitaine, vol. 6, fasc. 2, 1948 (1950), pp. 395 and 397–8.

'Lascaux, quelques vues personnelles', *Bulletin de la Société d'Études et de Recherches préhistoriques des Eyzies*, no. 3, 1953, pp. 19–22.

BREUIL, Abbé H., 'La Grotte de Lascaux', rapport lu à *l'Académie des Inscriptions et Belles-Lettres*, 11 October 1940. Périgueux, 1940.

'La Grotte de Lascaux (Dordogne)', *Bull. de la Soc. préhistorique française*, 1941, pp. 60–1.

'Une Altamira française: la caverne de Lascaux à Montignac (Dordogne)', *Comptes-rendus de l'Acad. des Inscr. et B.-L.*, 1941, pp. 347–76.

'La Cueva de Lascaux', *Atlantis*, 1941.

'Oui ... Lascaux est authentique', *Les Nouvelles littéraires*, 1180, 13 April 1950, or *Bull. de la Soc. préh. fr.*, 1950, pp. 355–63 (same text).

'A propos de Lascaux', *Man*, vol. LII, July 1952, pp. 110–11.

'Lettre à Monsieur le Directeur de l'Architecture à propos de l'aménagement de la grotte de Lascaux', *Bull. de la Soc. préh. fr.*, vol. XLIX, 1952, pp. 22–3.

'Lascaux', in *Quatre cents siècles d'art pariétal*, Montignac, 1952, pp. 106–51.

'La datation par C14 de Lascaux (Dordogne), at Philip Caves (S.W. Africa)', *SPF.*, vol. LI, fasc. 11–12, Dec. 1954, pp. 544–9.

BRODRICK, A. H., *Lascaux, a Commentary*, London, 1949.

CASTERET, Norbert, 'Lascaux Cave, Cradle of World Art', *Nat. Geogr. Mag.*, vol. 94, no. 6, 1948, pp. 771–94.

DANTHINE, Hélène, 'Essai d'interprétation de la "scène du puits" de la grotte de Lascaux', *Sédimentation et Quaternaire*, Compte-rendu du congrès tenu en Charente et Dordogne en 1949. Bordeaux, 1951, pp. 213–20.

ICHAC, Pierre, 'La Grotte à peintures de Montignac, en Dordogne', *L'Illustration*, Paris, 4 January 1941, pp. 9–16.

KOBY, 'Y a-t-il en à Lascoux un Bos longifrons?' *Bull. de la Soc. préh. fr.*, 1954, pp. 434–41.

LAMING, Annette, 'Un Sanctuaire paléolithique: la grotte de Lascaux', *L'Âge nouveau*, no. 30, 1948, pp. 63–9.

LAVAL, Léon, *La Caverne peinte de Lascaux*, Montignac, 1948.

LECHLER, George, 'The Interpretation of the "Accident Scene" at Lascaux', *Man*, vol. 51, December 1951, pp. 165–7.

MALVESIN-FABRE, 'La Grotte de Lascaux (Dordogne) et ses œuvres d'art préhistorique', *Préhistoire, Spéléologie ariégeoises*, VI, 1951, pp. 56–7.

'Le Symbolisme des peintures de Lascaux', *Sédimentation et Quaternaire*, Compte-rendu du Congrès tenu en Charente et Dordogne en 1949. Bordeaux, 1951, pp. 259–63.

MARTINEZ SANTA OLALLA, 'Neues über prähistorische Felsmalereien in Frankreich (Lascaux), Spanien (Gasulla-Schlucht, prov. Castellon) und Marokko (Yebd Kasba, Spanisch Marokko)', *IPEK*, vol. 15–16, 1941–2, pp. 1–24.

PEYRONY, D., 'L'Art pictural de la grotte de Lascaux et celui dit: "Levantin espagnol" ', *Bull. de la Soc. préh. fr.*, vol. XLVI, no. 3–4, April 1949, p. 117.

'L'Industrie de la grotte de Lascaux', *ibid.*, XLVII, 1950, pp. 136–7.

RÉALITÉS, 'Allez voir les maîtres de Lascaux', *Réalités*, February 1955, I, pp. 26–33.

ROCHE, Abbé J., 'La Grotte de Lascaux', *La Nature*, May 1951.

WINDELS, F., *Lascaux, chapelle sixtine de la préhistoire*, Montignac 1948. Texte de A. Laming, English transl. by C. F. C. Hawkes, London 1949.

ZEUNER, F. E., 'The Colour of the Wild Cattle of Lascaux', *Man*, May 1953, pp. 68–9.

INDEX